I0529096

Praise for

67 DAY YEAR

"*67 Day Year* is one of those books that helps you understand your blocks around success, setting goals, and having a mindset that gets results. Dr. Irvine is a leader who helps others grow and achieve more quickly. I highly recommend her work to anyone who wants to grow."

PAT FLYNN, Wall Street Journal bestselling author of *Will It Fly*

"Working on my mindset has been the single most important thing I've done to grow my business, and Dr. Shannon is a true expert in understanding the neuroscience behind achieving goals and business success. If you want to get results you didn't dare believe to be possible, start reading this book today."

JASMINE STAR, world-class speaker, thought leader, podcast host, CEO, and entrepreneur

"Dr. Shannon Irvine is the go-to when it comes to rewiring your mind for success. Her work is like a shortcut to turning on your success switch—helping you hack the patterns that hold you back and install the ones that move you forward. If you're ready to collapse the time it takes to hit your goals, *67 Day Year* is your roadmap."

CHRISTINA JANDALI, success coach, business growth strategist, and founder of Deliver Your Genius

67

DAY YEAR

3 SIMPLE STEPS to WIRE YOUR BRAIN
to ACHIEVE MORE in LESS TIME

DAY
YEAR

DR. SHANNON IRVINE

Copyright © 2025 Shannon Irvine
All rights reserved.

No part of this publication may be reproduced, distributed, or transmitted in any form or by
any means, including photocopying, recording, or other electronic or mechanical methods,
without the prior written permission of the publisher, except in the case of brief quotations
embodied in reviews and certain other noncommercial uses permitted by copyright law.

Mind Matrix™, Brain Prime™, STEBDAR™, and SINC Neuro Coaching Model™
are trademarks of Team Irvine LLC.

Paperback ISBN: 979-8-9923306-1-8
Hardcover ISBN: 979-8-9923306-2-5
eBook ISBN: 979-8-9923306-0-1

PSY020000   PSYCHOLOGY / Neuropsychology
SEL027000   SELF-HELP / Personal Growth / Success
BUS107000   BUSINESS & ECONOMICS / Personal Success

Cover design and typesetting by Kaitlin Barwick
Edited by Justin Greer

www.67dayyearbook.com

This book is dedicated to the dreamers—the change makers—the driven—the called. Those who don't think the status quo is to stay the same but to be changed. For those who know that "for such a time as this—they were born—to honor God" and to change lives for the better. For those who are willing with the arrows in their back to prove it—that you can do anything you put your brain to! For those who are ready to flip their brain's success switch to ON—and just maybe CHANGE THE WORLD!

Contents

Part One
Flip Your Brain's Success Switch ON

Contents

Part Two
The Tools

Contents

Part Three
The 67-Day Year Method

Contents

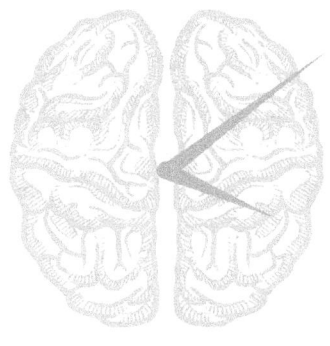

PART ONE

Flip Your Brain's Success Switch ON

How to Create a YEAR'S Results in Just 67 Days

"Once you learn to do something consciously, you can move it into the subconscious and do it well. Everything you do well will be done subconsciously."

Zig Ziglar

1

Achievement, *Accelerated*

Have you ever wondered why some people seem to sprint effortlessly toward their goals, dreams, and desires, achieving them almost as if by magic?

Take the story of Julia. Back in 2022, Julia found herself where many of us often do. Despite her high ambitions and relentless efforts, her entrepreneurial dreams always seemed just beyond her grasp. As a dedicated mom of twin girls who were starting to spend more time with friends, Julia saw an opportunity to turn her passion for health and fitness into a career. She launched a coaching business to help other moms stay fit while juggling all the craziness of parenthood.

Julia had big dreams. She wanted to help as many moms as possible, send her kids to an amazing high school, and take her family on yearly trips to exotic places, starting with a grand adventure in Europe. More than anything, she longed to give her family the financial security she never had growing up.

Determined to make it happen, Julia invested in online courses and got certified by a well-known celebrity coach. But here's the thing: those courses didn't really teach her the nitty-gritty of running a business, getting clients, marketing effectively, or delivering results that keep clients coming back for more. Even though she was showing up on Instagram Lives and diving into the wild world of TikTok, the response was . . . well, let's just say it was underwhelming. After months of pouring her heart into her business, the excitement of landing her first client fizzled out as the crickets started chirping in her inbox. Her optimism was fading fast. And that light of hope? It was dimming by the day.

Maybe you've been there too, pouring your heart and soul into your work, armed with every book and course you can get your hands on, but still coming up short. It's not like you're not trying—heck, you've probably achieved a ton already! But that dream of growing your business and seeing your vision take flight? Somehow, it stays just out of reach. You need to figure out a way to bridge the gap between what you have and what you want.

That's exactly what this book is all about. I'm going to help you figure out what's been holding you back and show you the exact steps to not only achieve your goals but also accomplish a year's worth of progress in just 67 days. Yep, you read that right—*67 days!*

This book? It's not just a guide. It's a game changer. It's about hitting the release button on the brakes that have been slowing you down so you can create mind-blowing results faster than you ever thought possible. You're about to tap into the most powerful operating system you've got: that incredible brain of yours. And I'm going to show you how to get it working *for* you, not against you. Together, we're going to flip your brain's "success switch" to ON and keep it there, setting you on a path of unprecedented achievement.

MY JOURNEY TO
THE 67-DAY YEAR

I'm Dr. Shannon Irvine, and my journey to creating the 67-Day Year started during one of the toughest, most eye-opening times of my life. I was feeling completely stuck; I had big dreams and tons of drive, but I felt like I was running in place. My charity, Mosaic Vision, was working overtime to support AIDS orphans in Uganda, with the goal of sponsoring a thousand kids. And as a business coach, I was deep in what I called "stressed success"— starting the day with coffee, ending with wine, and living by the "hustle and grind" mantra. But my health and personal life? They were paying the price.

Then, everything changed. I stared at the pregnancy test on my bathroom counter, a positive result shining back. The joy was unreal. After five years of hoping and praying, I was going to be a mom! But just as quickly, that joy mixed with fear. How was I going to balance being the mom I wanted to be with the career I'd built?

In the middle of all those swirling emotions, I had a light-bulb moment. As I watched the sunlight peeking through my window, warming the tears on my cheeks, I felt a nudge from above: Why not both? Why couldn't I be an amazing mom *and* a thriving entrepreneur? What if life wasn't about choosing either/or, but embracing "and"?

That one thought? It completely shattered my "either/or" mindset and kicked off a whole new era of "and." I started reimagining not just motherhood, but a life where all my callings could coexist and thrive. It required a whole new way of thinking, breaking free from the patterns that had brought me success but at a pretty hefty cost.

In my quest for balance, a pivotal question emerged: *What if life could be about "and" instead of "either/or"? What if I didn't have to sacrifice one dream for another?* This thought led me to seek inspiration from a mentor who embodied the "and" life I aspired to—a life of faith, family, and flourishing businesses.

I invested $50,000 for one-on-one coaching with her, driven by curiosity to uncover her "secret sauce." Surprisingly, I found that the strategies and tactics she used were similar to mine. The real difference was her mindset. She thought differently about money, success, worth, and service. Her approach was rooted in a deep belief in limitless potential, underpinned by faith and future-based thinking.

Limitless potential, underpinned by faith and future-based thinking.

As I spent more time with her, a profound shift began in my own mindset. I became fascinated with the power of thought. Why could she create such clarity and momentum while I struggled? This curiosity turned into an obsession, leading me to dive into scientific journals on synaptic pruning and brain plasticity. At the same time, scripture resonated deeply with me,

6

especially passages about renewing the mind and focusing on what is true, pure, and lovely.

Fueled by these aha moments, I started questioning all the traditional goal-setting and time-management models out there. They just don't cut it for our crazy, beautiful, complicated lives. This was a puzzle I had to solve. Deep down, I knew God created us for abundant lives, so I made a big pivot. I went from my business background to earning a PhD in neuropsychology, all to crack the code on how our brains achieve success.

Discovering the 67-Day Year Method

In my quest to understand how to achieve more without sacrificing what matters most, I uncovered a powerful truth: our brains are built for success, but we often get in our own way. Through my studies in neuropsychology, I developed the 67-Day Year method, a brain-based method which helps you wire your brain for achievement and accomplish your yearly goals in just over two months.

The key to having a 67-Day Year comes down to three big things:

1. **CLARIFY:** Get crystal clear on what you want and define success on your terms.
2. **ERASE:** Identify and eliminate the limiting beliefs that are holding you back.
3. **AUTOMATE:** Prime your brain for success and make your goals an inevitable part of your subconscious programming.

This method does more than provide a pathway to success; it collapses time, our most precious resource. When your brain fully embraces and believes in your direction, amazing things happen. You can achieve a year's worth of goals in just 67 days. This isn't just a hopeful promise; it's a reality that I've witnessed and am eager to share with you.

You can achieve a year's worth of goals in just 67 days.

UNLEASHING YOUR POTENTIAL

As I explored the power of thought and belief, I discovered a profound truth: how we think shapes our reality. The beliefs we hold about ourselves and our potential have an incredible impact on what we achieve. This understanding led me to dive deeper into the science of success and the role of our environment in shaping our beliefs.

Have you ever heard that we're the average of the five people we spend the most time with? This idea highlights the power of influence and belief. When we surround ourselves with individuals who believe in limitless potential and actively pursue growth, we profoundly shift our own beliefs and attitudes.

A study conducted with two groups of students illustrates this beautifully. One group was confident in their academic abilities, while the other was burdened by self-doubt. When placed in the same room for just twenty minutes without interaction, the doubting students' performance improved by 22 percent— simply by being in the presence of those who believed in their capabilities. This study shows that an environment where success and potential are embraced can significantly impact our own beliefs and performance.

By picking up this book, you're entering such an environment. You're challenging the limitations you've set for yourself and embarking on a journey of growth and limitless potential. You're tapping into the power of your brain, focused effort, and a mindset that aligns with God's promises.

Scripture reminds us to "think on what is good, true, pure, lovely, and praiseworthy" (Philippians 4:8) and to be "transformed by the renewal of your mind" (Romans 12:2). These passages beautifully align with scientific principles like neuroplasticity, which empower us to reshape our thoughts and actions toward success.

Your potential is not limited by your past or your current circumstances. God has created you for greatness, and by embracing the power of your mind and faith, you can unlock a life of extraordinary achievement and fulfillment.

Your potential is not limited by your past or your current circumstances.

Through my studies in neuropsychology, I developed the 67-Day Year method, which helps you rewire your brain for achievement and accomplish your yearly goals in just over two months. And in this book, I'll teach you how to do that.

I'll guide you through the exact steps that leverage how your brain naturally fosters success. I will show you how to unlock your true potential by identifying and eliminating the limiting beliefs that have been holding you back, paving the way for unhindered growth and achievement.

Remember, you are fully equipped. The success you envision as you drift off to sleep isn't just a dream. It's well within your grasp, waiting for you to *flip that success switch to ON*.

This process isn't about being extraordinary by conventional standards. I'm not some rare unicorn. This works because it aligns with how God created our brains for us to be successful. It taps into the science of transformation and achievement.

As you engage with the 67-Day Year method, you'll learn to identify and eliminate the limiting beliefs holding you back. You'll discover how to prime your brain for success, making your goals an inevitable part of your subconscious programming.

HERE'S WHAT LIES AHEAD

In the following chapters, you'll embark on a transformative journey that will reshape your approach to success and help you achieve your goals with unprecedented speed and clarity.

You'll learn how to:

- Convince your brain that chasing your dreams is safe.
- Align your subconscious with your vision.
- Identify and erase the limiting beliefs that have been holding you back, using powerful techniques to rewire your thought patterns.
- Automate your success by priming your brain's pathways and making your goals an inevitable part of your subconscious programming.

- Set and achieve your goals using the revolutionary 67-Day Year method, accomplishing more in just over two months than most people do in a year.

Each section of this book is interactive, with prompts that encourage you to apply what you're learning immediately. For those who want to dive deeper, a comprehensive workbook accompanies the text, along with video tutorials and additional resources available at www.67dayyearbook.com. These tools are designed to enhance your understanding and application of the 67-Day Year method, providing you with everything you need to transform your approach to success.

As you engage with this material, you're not just reading about change; you're beginning to live it. Step by step, you'll turn your aspirations into achievements, flipping your brain's success switch to ON and opening the door to a life of fulfilled potential. So turn the page and let's dive in. Your 67-Day Year starts now!

2

Rethinking Success

Beyond Hard Work and Goal Setting

Have you ever been told that success is as simple as setting a goal, working your tail off, and *voilà!* your dreams will magically come true? Sounds easy, right? But if that's the case, why are so many of us still chasing those dreams instead of living them? If you've ever found yourself pouring your heart and soul into your goals, only to feel like you're spinning your wheels, know that you're not alone.

Take Maya, for example. She's a corporate lawyer who bought into the idea that success meant burning the midnight oil. Despite her unwavering dedication, she found herself on the brink of burnout, questioning the true value of her achievements. Or Elijah, the aspiring tech entrepreneur who followed the textbook startup playbook—network, pitch, rinse, and repeat—only to watch his venture struggle to take off.

Then there's Sophia, who pursued academic success all the way to a PhD, only to find the job market oversaturated and opportunities scarce. And Carlos, the talented filmmaker who discovered that even with a killer reel and a tireless work ethic, breaking into the industry was an uphill battle without the right connections. Anita, a meticulous planner whose beautiful café was hit hard by an unexpected economic downturn, proves that even the best-laid plans can be derailed by forces beyond our control.

Do any of these stories resonate with you? Have you ever found yourself in a similar situation, wondering why your hard work and dedication haven't yielded the results you expected? If so, it's time to take a step back and question the conventional wisdom around success.

Even the best-laid plans can be derailed by forces beyond our control.

THE MYTHS AND MISCONCEPTIONS HOLDING YOU BACK

In our quest for success, we often cling to beliefs that seem to offer a clear path forward. However, many of these beliefs are actually myths and misconceptions that can hold us back from achieving our true potential. Let's debunk some of these pervasive ideas and uncover the truth hiding beneath the surface.

Hard Work Equals Success: We've all heard this one before: just put in the hours, and success will follow. But the reality is, hard work is just one piece of the puzzle. This belief ignores critical factors like timing, opportunity, and good old-fashioned luck. Too often, people find themselves burning the candle at both ends, only to end up disillusioned when their efforts don't yield the expected results. Success is more complex than simply working hard.

A College Degree Guarantees Success: There was a time when a college degree was seen as a one-way ticket to a successful career. But in today's world, where entrepreneurship and innovation reign supreme, a degree alone is no longer a golden ticket. Plenty of wildly successful people have forged their own paths, proving that real-world experience, skills, and a killer network can be just as valuable as a diploma. While education is important, it's not the only path to success.

SMART Goals Are the Blueprint for Success: Don't get me wrong, SMART goals (Specific, Measurable, Attainable, Relevant, and Time-bound) can be a helpful tool for clarifying your objectives. But the danger lies in getting so caught up in the rigidity of these goals that you miss out on unexpected opportunities or fail to adapt when circumstances change. Success often requires flexibility and the ability to pivot when needed.

Having Strategy-Based Mentors Is a Shortcut to Success: Having a mentor to guide you can be invaluable, but it's not a magic bullet. Your success depends on your own dedication, adaptability, and willingness to learn and grow. It also is dependent on how your brain is wired: *Is it wired to win and achieve?* Or is it on default— seeing any resistance as a reason to stop trying? A mentor's strategies might work wonders for them, but that doesn't mean they'll translate seamlessly to your unique situation. Mentors can light the way, but you must walk the path yourself.

Vision Boards and Affirmations Lead Directly to Success: Vision boards and affirmations can be great tools for staying motivated and focused, but they're not a substitute for action. You can't just wish your way to success. Vision boards and affirmations are supplements to, not substitutes for, the actual work required to achieve your dreams.

So where do these myths come from, and why do they have such a hold on us? The answer lies in a complex web of societal norms, cultural narratives, historical contexts, and psychological tendencies.

The American Dream

Let's start with "the American Dream." This powerful cultural narrative has shaped our understanding of success for generations, suggesting that anyone can make it big with enough hard work and determination, regardless of their background. It's an inspiring idea, but it glosses over the very real systemic inequalities and the role of privilege and luck in shaping outcomes.

The Meritocracy Myth

Closely tied to the American Dream is the idea of meritocracy—the notion that talent and effort are always rewarded. And while this can be a great motivator, it doesn't always account for the structural barriers that can prevent equal access to opportunities.

The Impact of the Industrial Revolution and Capitalism

The Industrial Revolution and the rise of capitalism also played a huge role in shaping our modern understanding of success. Suddenly, success wasn't just about noble titles or divine favor; it was something that could be earned through hard work and entrepreneurial spirit. But while this shift opened up new possibilities, it also tied success to wealth accumulation and productivity in a way that can feel restrictive and hollow.

Psychological Biases at Play

From a psychological standpoint, our tendency to believe in these myths is reinforced by cognitive biases like confirmation bias (seeking out information that confirms what we already believe) and the halo effect (assuming that someone who is successful in one area must be successful in all areas). And with the rise of social media, we're constantly bombarded with curated highlight reels that make success seem more attainable than it really is.

Recognizing the complex interplay of societal norms, cultural narratives, historical contexts, and psychological tendencies that shape our beliefs about success is a crucial step in breaking free from these myths and crafting our own definition of success—one that's authentic and fulfilling, one that aligns with our individual values and aspirations. By questioning the assumptions and biases that underlie our understanding of achievement, we can begin to blaze our own trail, equipped with the tools and mindset needed to thrive in this crazy, beautiful, ever-changing world.

Now, let's talk about why those traditional methods of goal achievement and hard work just don't cut it in today's world.

TRADITIONAL METHODS CAN'T MEET OUR MODERN CHALLENGES

Think back to your school days—the endless hours of memorization, the pressure to conform and follow the rules. Remember sitting with your hand up, waiting just to be heard? Those moments weren't just about patience and discipline; they were subtly teaching us to seek approval from others, to wait for permission, to quiet that bold inner voice guiding our way.

As we climbed the educational ladder, getting that perfect grade became the ultimate measure of success. But were we really learning to think for ourselves, or were we just getting really good at jumping through hoops? Think about it—weren't we just mirroring what the system wanted? Conforming to get that stamp of approval? Teachers, bless their hearts, were part of a system designed not for fostering our unique spark but more so for creating a well-oiled, rule-following machine.

Don't get me wrong, I'm not here to bash education. But it's important to recognize that the system was designed for a different era: the industrial age, a time when following instructions and fitting in were the keys to success. In today's rapidly evolving world, where innovation

The system was designed for a different era.

17

and creativity are the currencies of success, those old methods just don't hold up.

For starters, the breakneck pace of technological change means that the skills that are in demand today might be obsolete tomorrow. Traditional goal setting often fails to account for the need for adaptability and continuous learning that modern jobs require. If you're too rigidly focused on a specific set of goals, you might miss out on opportunities to adapt and learn new skills that could be a vital tipping point for your career.

There's also a growing recognition that success isn't just about climbing the corporate ladder or padding your bank account. More and more people are seeking work that aligns with their values and gives them a sense of purpose and ful-fillment. Traditional goal-setting methods that are laser-focused on quantifiable metrics like salary and job title just don't capture the full picture of what success means to many people today.

Success isn't just about climbing the corporate ladder or padding your bank account.

And don't even get me started on the toll that the "always on" culture of modern work can take on our well-being. When we're constantly plugged in and available, it's all too easy to fall into the trap of equating long hours with productivity and success. But as countless studies have shown, working longer doesn't necessarily mean working better. In fact, it can lead to burnout, decreased efficiency, and a host of negative health impacts.

A study by the World Health Organization in 2019 found that working 55 hours or more per week was associated with a 35 percent higher risk of stroke and a 17 percent higher risk of dying from heart disease compared to working 35–40 hours a week. If that's not a wake-up call to prioritize well-being in our pursuit of success, I don't know what is!

Oh, and let's not forget about the rise of the gig economy and the growing trend toward freelance and project-based work. In this new landscape, success is less about climbing a linear career ladder and more about building a diverse portfolio of skills and experiences that you can apply to a variety of projects and roles.

To thrive in this environment, you need to be able to pivot quickly, learn on the fly, and juggle multiple projects and deadlines. Traditional goal-achievement methods based on the idea of steady, long-term progress in a single role just don't translate well to this new reality.

The Shifting Definition of Success

At the same time, there's been a profound shift in how we think about work–life balance and what it means to be successful. The old model of success, where work always came first and personal life was an afterthought, is increasingly being rejected in favor of a more holistic approach that values well-being, relationships, and personal fulfillment alongside professional achievements.

This shift is being driven in part by a growing awareness of the negative impacts of stress and overwork on our physical and mental health, as well as a desire for a more meaningful and purposeful life outside of work. As a result, the definition of success is becoming more individualized, reflecting a broader range of personal values and priorities.

I've seen this shift firsthand in my business. More and more of my clients are coming to me not just with professional goals but with a deep desire to create a life that feels balanced, fulfilling, and aligned with their values. They're realizing that success isn't just about what they achieve but how they feel along the way.

In this new landscape, setting and achieving goals requires a different approach—one that is more adaptable, integrated, and self-aware. It's not just about hitting arbitrary milestones or following a prescribed path; it's about aligning your professional aspirations with your personal values and continuously evolving and growing in response to change.

Fortunately, there's a growing body of research and thought leadership that's shedding new light on what it takes to achieve success and fulfillment. Angela Duckworth's groundbreaking work on the power of grit and perseverance and Cal Newport's insights on the importance of deep, focused work are two endeavors of many by thinkers who are challenging conventional wisdom and offering new frameworks for thinking about success.

One of the key themes that emerges from this work is the importance of developing a growth mindset—the belief that our abilities and intelligence can be developed through effort and learning. This mindset is essential, as it allows us to embrace challenges and setbacks as opportunities for growth and learning.

Another theme is the importance of focusing on the things that matter most—the 20 percent of activities that drive 80 percent of results, as the Pareto Principle suggests. In a world of constant demands and distractions, the ability to prioritize and focus on the things that truly move the needle is more important than ever.

There's also a growing recognition of the importance of purpose and meaning in driving long-term success and fulfillment. As Simon Sinek argues in his work on the power of "why," individuals and organizations that are driven by a clear sense of purpose are more resilient, innovative, and successful over the long haul.

These insights collectively point toward a new approach to success—one that's grounded in self-awareness, adaptability, and a commitment to continuous growth and learning. Rather than blindly following a prescribed path or chasing arbitrary metrics, this approach invites us to get curious about what truly matters to us, embrace challenges as opportunities for growth, and stay open to new possibilities and ways of thinking.

So, where does all this leave us? If the traditional methods of goal setting and hard work are no longer enough in today's world, what's the alternative?

The answer lies in unlocking the incredible power of your own brain. By understanding how your brain responds to goals, stress, and motivation, you can develop strategies tailored to your unique strengths and challenges and harness the full potential of your mind to drive success and fulfillment.

The answer lies in unlocking the incredible power of your own brain.

THE BRAIN'S ROLE IN SUCCESS

The inner workings of your subconscious mind play a pivotal role in shaping your perceptions, decisions, and reactions to challenges. Understanding the brain's mechanisms—how it responds to goals, stress, and motivation—can dramatically transform your approach to achieving success.

The brain's response to goals is not just a matter of willpower or conscious effort; it involves a complex interplay between our cognitive functions and emotional centers. For example, setting goals that are aligned with our intrinsic values activates more positive, sustainable motivation compared to goals imposed by external pressures, like just making money. This alignment can enhance our focus, resilience, and satisfaction, leading to a more rewarding journey toward success.

I experienced this firsthand when I set a goal to write this book. At first, I was motivated by external factors like the potential for increased visibility and revenue. But as I dug deeper and connected with my core purpose of empowering others to live their best lives, I discovered a newfound sense of energy and commitment that sustained me through the challenges of the writing process. Aligning my goal with my values made all the difference.

Stress, on the other hand, has a profound impact on our ability to think clearly, make decisions, and stay motivated. Understanding the brain's stress response—how it can be both a hindrance and a motivator—is crucial. By managing stress effectively, you can use it to foster growth and resilience rather than allowing it to derail your aspirations.

In the next chapter, we'll dive deep into the inner workings of your subconscious mind—the true command center of your thoughts, beliefs, and actions. We'll uncover how the subconscious mind influences your behavior and goal setting processes. By learning to tap into and program your subconscious beliefs and habits, you can overcome self-imposed limitations and navigate toward your goals with greater ease and confidence. No more chasing arbitrary metrics or following outdated formulas—this is about creating a path that is uniquely tailored to your strengths, values, and aspirations.

We'll also explore how your subconscious shapes your reality in ways that you may not even be aware of and how you can tap into its power to accelerate your progress toward your goals. Get ready to break free from the slow, tedious grind and step into a life where your goals don't just happen—they happen at lightning speed!

3

The Power of Belief

Harnessing the Subconscious Mind

Did you know that your subconscious mind is the true mastermind behind your decisions, actions, and overall success? It's like having a hidden superhero living right inside your brain, working tirelessly to shape your reality. Your subconscious mind holds all your beliefs, memories, skills, and experiences, constantly influencing your daily decisions and behaviors without you even realizing it.

Think about how you learn to drive. At first, it requires all your focus, but after a while, driving becomes second nature. You can navigate the roads without consciously thinking about every action because your subconscious has taken over. The same goes for habits—the things you do every day without really deciding to, like grabbing a coffee first thing in the morning, are driven by your subconscious. It's following a familiar pattern, one that has been deeply ingrained through repetition and past experiences.

Just as your subconscious can work in your favor by automating tasks and habits, it can also work against you when it comes to your beliefs about success. Your subconscious beliefs can trip you up on your path to success. If, deep down, you don't believe you can be successful or deserve it, these hidden beliefs can sabotage your efforts, causing you to procrastinate or not give your all. Even if you consciously know that improving certain skills, like public speaking, could benefit you, your subconscious might make you want to avoid it because it associates the activity with fear or anxiety.

Your subconscious beliefs can trip you up on your path to success.

Despite the significant impact of the subconscious mind on our daily lives and overall success, it has often been overlooked or misunderstood. For too long, the subconscious has been the unsung hero—the hidden treasure that many overlook. But brain science has a lot to say about this mighty powerhouse, and it's brimming with untapped potential.

Your brain possesses an incredible ability called neuroplasticity, which allows it to change and strengthen certain thought patterns over time. The more you think something, the easier it becomes to think that way again. That's how a repeated thought can become a deep-seated belief without you consciously deciding to believe it. These thinking habits can be beneficial or detrimental, depending on what you've learned from the people and world around you.

Conditioning is one way you learn these habits. It's like when you hear a song that reminds you of a fun summer, and you instantly feel happy without consciously trying to think about that summer. That song has become linked to your happy memory. Similarly, your repeated thoughts and feelings about your experiences can gradually turn into beliefs you hold about yourself or the world.

Understanding how your subconscious works gives you an opportunity to change it for the better. By recognizing the deep-rooted beliefs that control your actions and decisions, you can start to align your hidden beliefs with your goals, propelling you closer to your dreams. The tools you'll learn in this book will teach you the exact steps to do so, helping you grow and succeed in new ways. I bet I know what you are thinking: "This has to be hard. Isn't working with the subconscious 'sciencey'?" Good news: it is a step-by-step, recipe-like process of adding and removing—one that is so easy, if you can build a house with those big chunky LEGOs, this will be a breeze! That's the most surprising part: everyone CAN do this . . . but most won't.

BELIEFS AND MINDSET: THE GUIDING FORCES

Your beliefs and mindset are incredibly important because they guide your actions, decisions, and overall success. Essentially, your beliefs are the things you're convinced are true, stemming from your family, experiences, and learning. Your mindset is how you view the world—whether you believe you can improve your abilities (growth mindset) or think your abilities are fixed and cannot change (fixed mindset).

Sometimes, your brain takes shortcuts in thinking, called cognitive biases, which aren't always accurate. For example, confirmation bias makes you pay more attention to information that agrees with what you already believe, even if there's evidence suggesting you might be wrong. This can make you stuck in your ways and unable to see the whole picture. Another example is the self-fulfilling prophecy, where your beliefs influence your actions, making your beliefs come true. If you think you're bad at math, you might not study much, get a poor grade, and then think, "See, I knew I was bad at math," even though you could have improved with more practice.

The placebo effect demonstrates how powerful your beliefs can be. If people believe they're receiving medicine (even if it's just a sugar pill), they can feel better simply because they think they're being treated. It's all about the strong influence of belief on your health and happiness. People who believe they can learn and grow are more likely to take on new challenges and excel in their careers compared to those who think their abilities are fixed and cannot be changed. Successful athletes, for example, often believe they can win and see challenges as opportunities to improve. This mindset helps them perform well.

Pause for a moment and reflect on your beliefs. Consider where they came from and how they affect your choices. Look back at a recent choice you made because of your biases. What did you ignore because it didn't fit with your beliefs? This exercise can help you understand how biases shape your decisions. If you find a belief that's holding you back, try to see it differently. For instance, if you're scared of talking in front of people, tell yourself, "I can get better at public speaking with practice."

TRANSFORMING YOUR SUBCONSCIOUS FOR SUCCESS

Scientific research confirms that somewhere between 80 and 90 percent of your daily decisions, and therefore your actions and results, are driven by your subconscious mind. That's right—not the logical, thinking part of your brain but the part that operates below the surface. Your subconscious mind is like a hidden director of your life, holding onto all the beliefs, habits, and values you've picked up over the years, starting from when you were a kid. It's like a script that runs in the background, guiding how you see the world, how you react to things that happen, and how you make decisions.

Up to 90 percent of your daily decisions are driven by your subconscious mind.

You don't just wake up one day with these beliefs. They form over time from what you see, hear, and experience. Your family, friends, culture, and even school teach you these things without you realizing it. For example, if you grew up in a family where money was tight, you might start to think making a lot of money is really hard or not possible for you. This kind of thinking can affect how you feel about money and success later in life.

Your subconscious mind influences you in many ways, deciding how you act, how you feel, and how you view relationships. If you think you're not good enough, you might not try new things or take on challenges that could help you grow. If you always try to make others happy, you might say yes to things even when you don't want to, just because you think it's expected. Your deep beliefs can also change how you feel about things that happen to you and affect your relationships.

The great news? *Transforming your subconscious is simpler than you think.* It can be shifted in four simple steps. Imagine building your ideal subconscious with big, colorful LEGOs—straightforward, fun, and incredibly effective. You can create a subconscious that is 100 percent aligned with what you want, aligning 90 percent of your brain's automatic functioning with your true desires and driving you toward your goals on autopilot.

That is flipping on your brain's success switch. It's about rewiring your subconscious to work for you, not against you. And when you do that, you unlock a whole new world of potential and possibility. You start to harness the incredible power of belief and speed, propelling you toward your dreams faster than you ever thought possible.

Harnessing Belief and Speed

Imagine you're gearing up to traverse the vast landscapes of Canada, the wilderness of the United States, or the beautiful outback of Australia. Sure, there are countless ways to make this journey, but not all are equally efficient.

I have a friend who adores antique cars. He decided to take an epic trip across the United States in an old Volkswagen bus, charmed by its nostalgic vibe. It's a cool ride, no doubt, but here's the catch: the old bus's top speed was a leisurely 35 miles per hour. As he chugged across the country, every mile was a testament to patience and endurance. Yes, he made it from California to New York, but the journey was long and exhausting—and it took him six times longer than it would have if he had traveled with the speed and efficiency of a sleek Ferrari.

I can't help but think of the Israelites' journey in Scripture, wandering the desert for forty years when it should have been an eleven-day trip. Just like using an old VW for a cross-country trip, clinging to outdated, slow methods isn't going to cut it in our fast-paced world—and it's why you aren't making the progress you want.

The speed at which we pursue our goals is heavily influenced by our subconscious mind and the beliefs we hold. When we're weighed down by limiting beliefs and doubts, it's like driving that old VW bus—we may eventually reach our destination, but the journey is slow and arduous. On the other hand, when we're free from these mental constraints, we can accelerate toward our goals with the speed and efficiency of a Ferrari.

This is where the power of belief comes into play. Our subconscious mind, which holds our deepest beliefs and influences our actions, can either propel us forward or hold us back. When we have unwavering faith in our abilities and potential, we can achieve remarkable things with incredible speed.

A Fearless Approach: Jordan's Story

Let me tell you about the incredible speed our brains are capable of, and I've got the perfect example—my daughter, Jordan. When she was just thirteen months old, barely able to peek over her playpen, she somehow managed to pull herself out. That was just the start of her adventurous spirit.

As she grew, whether it was mastering the jungle gym or scaling a warped wall at her birthday party, Jordan always had her sights set on the next thrilling challenge. She had this unshakable belief, a confidence that she could conquer anything she set her mind to. This belief propelled her forward with remarkable speed.

Here's what's fascinating—when kids like Jordan haven't yet learned to fear or doubt, they tackle challenges with incredible energy and velocity. They don't have that mental picture of failure holding them back. It's a powerful lesson for us all. Often, it's not about amping up our belief but more about not letting doubt overshadow it.

You're always in a state of belief—either in your potential or your doubts. One attracts success; the other repels it. If we believe we can do great things and see challenges as chances to get better, we're more likely to try hard, keep going when things get tough, and find new ways to solve problems.

You're always in a state of belief—either in your potential or your doubts.

But if we're always doubting ourselves and think we can't get better, we might not even try new things. We might give up easily and miss out on some opportunities. Our actions reflect what we believe inside, whether we're reaching for our dreams or just watching them from afar.

Psychologists and brain scientists have found out a lot about how our beliefs form and how we can change them. Our brains can change and grow through neuroplasticity. This means that with some effort, we can start to think differently—and both science and spiritual teachings tell us that changing our thoughts can change our lives.

Changing what we believe deep down is possible. We can teach our brain to form new, positive pathways. Jordan's story, and what we all can experience, shows us that believing in ourselves in tough times can make a huge difference. Choosing to focus on our potential and keeping a positive mindset helps us move toward success and opens up a world of possibilities. This decision, supported by both faith and science, gives us the strength to face challenges with hope and keep working toward our dreams.

THE INCREDIBLE SPEED OF YOUR BRAIN

Let's talk numbers for a second. Your brain processes over 60,000 thoughts daily. Imagine if you had to consciously address each one! Thankfully, our brains have an incredible automation system where repeated thoughts get embedded into our subconscious, becoming our default mode.

When you repeat a thought about 40 to 67 times, something incredible happens in your brain. It's like your brain perks up and goes, "Hey, you seem to be really into this thought. You've been repeating it a lot. I'm taking that as a sign that it's important to you." So what does your amazing brain do next? It starts this process called glucose patterning. This is your brain's way of saying, "I've got this. I'll handle it from here."

This repeated thought is then shifted from your conscious, thinking mind right into your memory systems, nestled in the powerful limbic system. We often refer to this as the subconscious or "under conscious" part of the mind. This transition is phenomenal news, and here's why: that fantastic autopilot feature is like having the most advanced software running in the background of our minds, handling the heavy lifting of thought processing. This means we can focus on what truly matters, on those thoughts that align with our purpose and calling, while our brain efficiently takes care of the rest. Isn't that just remarkable? It's like having a divine personal assistant inside our heads, making sure we're always on track with what we believe and value!

Here's the challenge: did you know that your prefrontal cortex, the decision-making part of the brain, is fully developed at around twenty-one for females and twenty-four for males? So, much of what's in your subconscious was formed before you even had the full capacity to make deliberate choices. That means the key to unlocking your potential lies in reprogramming those automated thoughts.

Your brain's subconscious system is built for efficiency and speed, and guess what? You're in the driver's seat. You are the creator of your thoughts, and these thoughts shape your life, your experiences, your future. It's not about the goals you set or the affirmations you recite; it's about the thoughts you repeat and embed into your subconscious.

Isn't it time to flip your brain's success switch ON so you can have the success you've always dreamed of? Let's jumpstart your subconscious and see just how fast you can go!

BREAKING FREE FROM THE LIMITS OF
PAST EXPERIENCES AND BELIEFS

Our ingrained beliefs and thought patterns significantly shape our reality, often operating beneath the conscious level of our awareness. These beliefs serve as "internal governors," subtly yet powerfully dictating the pace and direction of our journey toward success and fulfillment. It's an intriguing concept that these subconscious beliefs, much like external mechanisms and self-imposed limitations, can restrict our progress and momentum.

Let me share with you a story that perfectly encapsulates this idea. You see, I'm a bit of a competitive soul. I've always had this inner drive, a kind of fiery competitiveness that constantly nudges me to be my absolute best. It's like an internal compass always pointing me toward improvement. And then there's my best friend—oh boy, talk about competitive! She's the kind of person who turns everything into a challenge—even something as mundane as brushing teeth becomes a race for her. It's just wired into her DNA.

So, there we were at a charity golf event, both of us with our competitive spirits in full swing. We were there not just for the thrill of the game, but for a cause close to our hearts—raising funds for our incredible organization Mosaic Vision. Right from the start, she's all pumped up, declaring she'll beat me by five strokes. We're neck and neck, mirroring each other's moves— she scores a birdie, I score a birdie; she's plus one, I'm plus one. And I knew if we were tied at the end, she'd want to race or something to determine who won.

As we approached the final hole, the excitement was tan- gible. She was certain victory was hers after she sank another birdie, but the round finished in a tie. And just as I had antici-pated, she turned to me and said, "Okay, let's race. Whoever gets to the restaurant first wins the tournament!" She was raring for a race to the finish line, winner takes all.

But here's the twist—I had a secret up my sleeve. What she didn't know was that my golf cart didn't have a governor. You see, a governor is that nifty little device that keeps the golf cart from speeding. Even if you push the gas pedal to the floor, that governor will not let you go more than five miles per hour. It's like the invisible hand that says, "Slow down, there's no rush." Her club-owned cart had one. But mine? It was free from those constraints. It was ready to fly.

Off she went, full throttle, but her cart was held back by the governor, crawling at a snail's pace. Meanwhile, I zoomed past her, the wind in my hair, freedom at my fingertips. Her face was a picture of disbelief and playful frustration as she flapped her arms, her competitive spirit still shining bright.

This little escapade with my golf cart is more than just a fun story. It's a metaphor for how we often hold ourselves back with invisible governors—limitations based on past experiences, beliefs about money, worth, confidence, and more. These are ingrained from our childhood, family, and societal influences long before our prefrontal cortex is fully developed. They're like invisible speed limits, subtly dictating how far and fast we can go. These governors slow us down, keeping us from reaching our true potential.

Okay, let's have a real-talk moment here. I'm willing to bet that right now, you're having one of those "aha" moments. You're probably thinking, "So that's why I hit a ceiling with my income! That's why I can get only so far with certain things. And when I step into uncharted territory, hello, self-doubt!" I hear you. It's like hitting a wall every time you try to push beyond your comfort zone, right?

These patterns, these frustrating loops we find ourselves in, they're not just random occurrences. Nope, they're deeply ingrained pathways carved out by the repetition of our past experiences. It's your brain doing what it does best—playing it safe, keeping you in familiar territory, wrapping you in a cozy blanket of "the known." But here's the kicker: if you want to grow, to really stretch and reach for those stars, you need to step into the unknown. You want to start that business, make an impact, live that dream? Well, sweet one, that means stepping off the well-trodden path and venturing into uncharted territory.

If you want to grow, to really stretch and reach for those stars, you need to step into the unknown.

And guess what? When you do that, your brain goes into full-on "Danger! Danger!" mode. It's like the internal alarm bells start ringing, red lights flashing, all systems on DEFCON level "Abort mission!" But here's what you need to know—and I want you to hear this loud and clear: It's not your fault. That's right, not your fault at all.

Remember, your brain has been wired from your past experiences—it's soaked up all those old stories about money, worth, what's enough, commitment, and potential. It's been marinating in a cocktail of fear, overwhelmed feelings, perfectionism, procrastination, and self-doubt. And now, it's operating on those outdated scripts, those old automations that just don't serve the magnificent, goal-smashing, dream-achieving you.

So what do we do about this? How do we rewire that super-smart brain of yours to align with your aspirations? How do we convince it that it's safe to soar, to explore, and to conquer new heights? That's what we're going to dive into next. We're going to learn how to override the old programming and install some brand-new, supercharged belief systems that will have you racing toward your goals like never before. Get ready, because your journey to a life of limitless potential starts now!

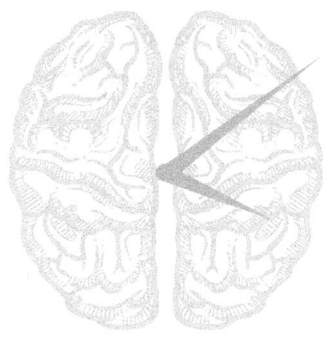

PART TWO

The Tools

Hardwire Your Brain for Success

4

The STEBDAR Model

Unlocking the Brain's Potential

Get ready for a transformative shift—we're upgrading from the familiar to the phenomenal! Buckle up, because I'm about to introduce you to a groundbreaking model that will revolutionize how you achieve your goals. Meet STEBDAR™, the foundation of the SINC Neuro Coaching Model™ I crafted while assembling the puzzle pieces of my own experiences.

STEBDAR isn't just a clever acronym; it's an innovative approach grounded in neuroscience, designed to shed light on how your brain processes information and translates it into actions. This model is incredibly effective for coaches, therapists, and anyone looking to instigate profound, lasting change in their lives.

Here's a breakdown of each component in the STEBDAR model, which represents a crucial step in how our brains manage, analyze, and ultimately utilize information to sculpt our realities:

Situation	This initiates our sensory perception—think of it as the spark that lights up our neural circuits.
Thoughts	These frame our interpretation of the event, shaping our perspective through a lens crafted by both divine wisdom and personal experience.
Emotions	Our feelings color these experiences, adding depth and texture to our interpretation.
Beliefs	These are the bedrock of our worldview, deeply rooted in our faith and understanding of our capabilities.
Decisions	Influenced by our beliefs, these are the critical choices that chart our course forward.
Actions	These are the tangible steps we take, driven by our decisions—a faithful step forward can move mountains.
Results	The outcomes of our actions, which then influence our future situations, creating a cycle of continuous growth and improvement.

By understanding and applying the STEBDAR model, we can begin to see how our interpretation of neutral situations—and the subsequent thoughts, emotions, beliefs, decisions, and actions we engage in—shapes our reality. This awareness empowers us to actively influence our thought patterns and behaviors, steering our lives toward more positive and fulfilling outcomes.

BREAKING DOWN STEBDAR

Situations (S)

The first component of our STEBDAR model, "Situations," challenges us to see beyond our initial reactions. It's a difficult but liberating concept. While emotionally charged events might seem inherently positive or negative, their true nature is detached. They are simply occurrences or circumstances that don't carry inherent meanings; the significance we give to them comes from our personal interpretations and reactions.

Situations are neutral because they exist outside of our thoughts, emotions, and beliefs. It is our perception—shaped by our past experiences, our expectations, and even our cultural and spiritual backgrounds—that assigns value and meaning to these events. Understanding this is crucial for realizing how we can wield power over our responses, instead of being controlled by external circumstances.

Consider the example of a sudden downpour:

Person A views the rain as a blessing, a welcome relief after a prolonged drought, interpreting it as an answer to prayers and a sign of renewal.

Person B, who had planned an outdoor gathering, sees the same rain as a calamity, feeling frustration and a sense of personal setback.

The rain itself is neutral; it simply falls as part of the natural world, without intent or emotion. It's the interpretation that changes, influenced by individual perceptions and contexts. This perspective shift allows us to approach life's events with a more objective viewpoint, potentially reducing the immediacy of emotional reactions.

For example, receiving criticism at work can initially feel harsh. Yet, if we view the feedback as neutral, it becomes something we can interpret constructively as an opportunity for growth, informed by our faith and values, or as something less personal and more about external circumstances.

This understanding encourages us to view life's situations not just as obstacles or blessings but as neutral events that provide opportunities for growth, understanding, and even deeper faith. By recognizing the neutrality of situations, we empower ourselves to choose our responses deliberately, aligning our actions with our values and the divine guidance we seek.

> *By recognizing the neutrality of situations, we empower ourselves to choose our responses deliberately.*

Thoughts (T)

Our brains are incredibly adept at producing thoughts that precede and shape our emotional landscapes. Before we experience any emotion about a situation, our minds are already busy at work. They perform a cognitive appraisal—this is where we interpret the situation based on our past experiences, beliefs, and attitudes, matching new information against our existing knowledge and beliefs to form specific thoughts about the situation. These thoughts then directly influence our emotions. So, if a situation is perceived as threatening, our brain might generate thoughts that lead to feelings of fear or anxiety. If it's seen as beneficial, our thoughts may shift toward happiness or excitement.

Imagine you're about to enter a job interview. The situation itself is neutral, an opportunity to meet potential employers and showcase your abilities. However, the thoughts that precede the interview can vary widely:

Positive Thought	"I'm well prepared and have the right qualifications for this role. I've succeeded before, and I can do it again."
Emotional Response	Confidence and calmness, fostering a sense of readiness.
Behavior	You approach the interview with a positive demeanor, respond to questions confidently, and engage dynamically with the interviewers.
Negative Thought	"I'm probably not as qualified as other candidates. What if I can't answer their questions?"
Emotional Response	Anxiety and self-doubt, which can cloud your presence.
Behavior	You might come across as nervous, hesitate in your responses, or fail to leave a strong impression.

In this example, while the situation—the job interview—remains constant, the thoughts about it drive vastly different emotions and behaviors. The first thought pattern promotes a positive and proactive response, potentially enhancing your interview performance. The second can hinder it, underscoring how pivotal our thoughts are in shaping our emotional and subsequent behavioral outputs.

Recognizing that thoughts precede emotions gives us a formidable tool to manage our emotional responses more effectively.

By becoming more aware of our thought patterns, especially those that are negative or irrational, we can influence our emotions and, consequently, our actions.

Emotions (E)

Emotions are far from random; they are intricate responses to our thoughts, crafted by a blend of neurochemicals like dopamine, serotonin, and norepinephrine. These chemicals stir into action based on our cognitive appraisals—essentially, the way we think about situations profoundly influences how we feel about them. These feelings, in turn, play a crucial role in shaping our beliefs about what we are capable of achieving, thus impacting the decisions we make.

> Emotions are far from random; they are intricate responses to our thoughts.

Our brains respond to thoughts by releasing specific neurochemicals that create our emotional states. Consider the following:

Dopamine is often linked with pleasure and reward. Think of the joy you feel when anticipating a positive event or achieving a goal—this is dopamine at work, enhancing your satisfaction.

Serotonin affects mood regulation. When you entertain positive, affirming thoughts, your serotonin levels may rise, promoting feelings of wellbeing and contentment.

Norepinephrine, associated with the body's fight-or-flight response, triggers feelings of arousal and alertness, especially when you perceive a situation as challenging or threatening.

Imagine you're preparing for a public speech:

Thought	"I've prepared thoroughly for this speech. My message is important and will resonate with the audience."
Emotion	Confidence and excitement, fueled by a dopamine surge in anticipation of a positive reception.
Behavior	Your delivery is enthusiastic and persuasive, capturing the audience's attention effectively.

Or let's say you're receiving constructive criticism:

Thought	"This feedback is an opportunity to learn and grow. Everyone has room for improvement."
Emotion	Gratitude and openness, possibly linked to increased serotonin levels, which help maintain a positive mood despite the challenge.
Behavior	You respond positively to the feedback, seeking clarity and ways to implement the suggestions.

Maybe you're facing a deadline at work:

Thought	"This deadline is daunting. I'm worried about letting my team down."
Emotion	Anxiety and stress, driven by norepinephrine, preparing your body to tackle the perceived threat.
Behavior	This stress might lead to procrastination or scattered work patterns, affecting your performance negatively.

Understanding that emotions directly stem from our thoughts offers a potent tool for personal development. By intentionally guiding our thoughts toward more positive frameworks or reframing negative situations, we can alter our emotional reactions. This shift not only influences our beliefs about our abilities but also impacts the choices we make, paving the way for more favorable outcomes in our personal and professional lives.

The "Emotions" component of STEBDAR highlights the significant influence our thoughts exert over our feelings and behaviors. By mastering this aspect, we can more effectively navigate our emotional landscapes, leading to improved wellbeing and greater success.

Beliefs (B)

Beliefs are the powerful blend of thoughts and emotions, intensified through repetition, much like a thought–emotion smoothie that strengthens with every blend. After about 67 repetitions— these patterns are deeply ingrained in your subconscious. This process results in beliefs that drive nearly 90 percent of your daily decisions, actions, and results.

The journey to belief formation starts when specific thoughts, paired with emotional responses, are repeatedly experienced. At around the "67 repeats" mark, these thought–emotion patterns begin to solidify into beliefs and shift to autopilot within the subconscious. Repetition reinforces neural pathways, making certain patterns more dominant. As these patterns automate, they settle into our subconscious, acting as default settings that govern our behavior and decision-making without our active awareness.

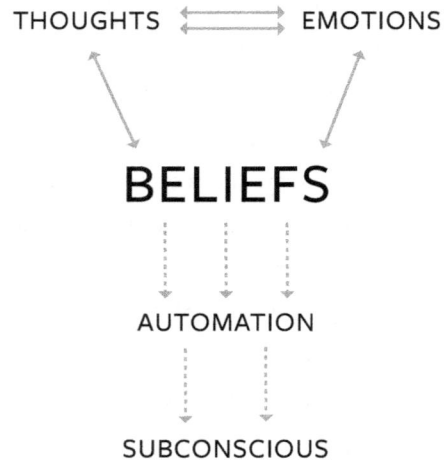

Let's break down a few examples of this process in different situations:

Professional Growth

You receive a promotion and are now in charge of an entire department. They are looking to you for leadership, and you want to excel at your job or new position.

Thought/ Emotion Pattern	Facing new work challenges with the mindset "I can handle this," paired with a surge of determination.
Belief Formation	After repeatedly overcoming challenges with this attitude, you cultivate a robust belief in your capabilities and resilience.
Impact	This belief propels a proactive approach to your new position and enhances your professional growth and success.

Public Speaking

An entrepreneur gets an opportunity to speak on stage to a thousand people for the first time.

Thought/ Emotion Pattern	Experiencing anxiety with repeated thoughts of "I'm terrible at this."
Belief Formation	If unaddressed, these thoughts and emotions solidify into a belief in your inherent inability to speak effectively in public.
Impact	This belief may cause you to shun speaking engagements, stunting personal and professional development.

Health and Fitness

You have decided right after the holidays to finally get in shape. You buy a gym membership and tell your best friend, who has decided to go with you on this journey.

Thought/ Emotion Pattern	Each workout ends with thoughts like, "I feel fantastic and strong," coupled with feelings of accomplishment.
Belief Formation	This recurring pattern fosters a belief that exercise is both rewarding and essential.
Impact	Motivated by this belief, you consistently engage in physical activities, boosting your health and vitality.

Recognizing that beliefs are forged from repeated thought and emotion patterns opens a pathway to transformative change. By employing tools from the SINC Neuro Coach Model, such as Brain Prime™ and the Mind Matrix™, you can intentionally alter these patterns. By challenging negative thoughts, fostering positive emotions, and practicing new behaviors, you reshape your beliefs. This change, in turn, affects your decisions, actions, and ultimately, the trajectory of your life.

The "Beliefs" stage of STEBDAR vividly shows how our cognitive and emotional patterns not only shape but can transform our reality. By mastering scientifically based tools for belief transformation, we can direct our lives in ways that resonate with our deepest values and aspirations, demonstrating how profoundly our inner world influences our external experiences.

Decisions, Actions, Results (DAR)

A significant portion of our daily decisions and actions, around 90 percent, are driven by the subconscious part of the brain. The prefrontal cortex—our center for logical thinking—is continually interacting with this automated system, drawing upon a reservoir of ingrained beliefs to navigate the complexities of life.

Decisions

Our decisions are deeply influenced by our beliefs, which frame our understanding of what is possible, desirable, and achievable. When we are faced with choices, our brain consults these beliefs to evaluate the options. This process often occurs below the level of conscious awareness and directs the paths we choose to take. For example, if you hold a firm belief that hard work leads to success, you are more likely to decide to take on additional projects at work, seeing them as opportunities for advancement.

Actions

The decisions we make based on our beliefs directly lead to our actions. These actions are the tangible manifestations of our decisions, embodying our commitment to the paths we've chosen. Continuing from the previous example, deciding to embrace more work might lead you to stay late at the office, work over the weekends, or invest in professional development courses. These actions are driven by the underlying belief in the value of hard work and its correlation with success.

Results

The results are the natural outcomes of our actions, which are themselves the product of the decisions shaped by our beliefs. These outcomes then feed back into our belief system, either reinforcing our existing beliefs or prompting us to reconsider them based on the new experiences. For instance, if your increased efforts at work lead to a promotion, it reinforces the belief that hard work pays off. Conversely, if the outcome is not as expected, it might lead to questioning this belief.

Consider the shift to remote work as an everyday example that shows DAR in action. Some people might embrace the thought that remote work offers a fantastic opportunity for work–life balance, leading to feelings of optimism. This belief that remote work enhances personal wellbeing might lead to decisions like creating a structured daily routine that balances work tasks with personal activities. The actions taken—such as setting up a dedicated workspace at home and scheduling regular breaks for exercise or hobbies—result in increased satisfaction with work–life balance and possibly improved productivity. These outcomes reinforce the belief in the benefits of remote work.

Conversely, those who view the shift to remote work with apprehension, worrying about isolation and decreased productivity, may experience feelings of anxiety. Their belief that remote work could negatively impact their work dynamics leads to decisions aimed at enhancing connection with colleagues. Actions like initiating virtual coffee breaks or participating in online professional development might vary in effectiveness, with the results either alleviating concerns or reinforcing initial apprehensions.

Understanding the STEBDAR model equips us to navigate life more deliberately, moving from passive experience to active creation. By recognizing the influence of subconscious beliefs on our decisions and actions, we can consciously align our beliefs with our desired outcomes, profoundly impacting both our personal and professional lives.

EMBRACING THE STEBDAR MODEL

Applying the STEBDAR model to personal growth and goal achievement is a conscious, step-by-step endeavor that can profoundly reshape your life's trajectory. This methodical approach begins by dissecting and understanding each component—Situations, Thoughts, Emotions, Beliefs, Decisions, Actions, and Results—allowing you to craft a tailored action plan for self-improvement.

Step 1: Identify the Situation

First, consider a current challenge or goal and reflect deeply on it. Describe this situation in neutral terms to emphasize that it is not the situation itself, but your response to it, that you can control. Ask yourself, "What are the factual aspects of this situation, stripped of any emotional or interpretive bias?" This step sets the foundation for a clear-minded approach to your challenge.

Step 2: Examine Your Thoughts

Next, jot down your initial thoughts about this situation. These are often automatic thoughts that surface without much deliberate consideration. Evaluate whether these thoughts are aiding or obstructing your progress toward your goal. This analysis helps you identify and modify unhelpful patterns early in the process.

Step 3: Acknowledge Your Emotions

Moving forward, identify and label the emotions that arise from your thoughts. It's important to accept these emotions without judgment, acknowledging them as valid responses to your thoughts. Consider how these emotions influence your behavior and decision-making. This awareness is crucial as it highlights the emotional underpinnings that may need addressing to change your behavior effectively.

Step 4: Uncover the Underlying Beliefs

The fourth step involves digging deeper to uncover the underlying beliefs that drive your thoughts and emotions. Look for patterns that might reveal core beliefs about yourself, others, or the world. Challenge yourself with questions like, "What beliefs are driving my thoughts and emotions in this situation? Which of these are blocking my desired outcomes?" This introspection can be aided by tools like the Mind Matrix to apply a Truth Prime, which helps in pruning obstructive beliefs. We will cover these tools in the following chapters.

We all have three core needs that our beliefs are trying to align with: Am I safe? Am I enough? Am I worthy? Ask yourself, "What thought does my brain tell me in each of the areas I am wanting to grow in?" Your brain is always trying to keep you where you are right now, right here. Your brain will only allow you to access what will keep you safe and familiar. So, what is your brain telling you about your future goals? What thoughts are arising? Are you hearing that you are not enough, that you don't have what it takes, or who would listen to you? Identifying beliefs that are keeping you stuck is the first step to removing them.

Identifying beliefs that are keeping you stuck is the first step to removing them.

Step 5: Decide

With a clearer understanding of how your beliefs affect your decisions, consciously decide if you need to change your approach based on a more constructive belief system. Think about the decisions you would make if your beliefs were fully aligned with your goals. This decision-making process is pivotal as it directly influences the actions you will take next.

Step 6: Take Action

Outline specific actions that reflect your new decisions and beliefs. These actions should be small, measurable, and achievable to ensure they are manageable and lead to real change. Ask yourself, "What's the first step I can take right now that aligns with my desired outcome?" This step translates your decisions into tangible actions.

Step 7: Observe the Results

After implementing your actions, take time to reflect on the results. Did the change in thoughts, emotions, and beliefs lead to a different outcome than before? Analyzing these results allows you to see the effectiveness of your changes and adjust as necessary. This reflection is vital for continuous improvement and for reinforcing positive changes.

IMPLEMENTING THE ACTION PLAN

To fully integrate the STEBDAR model into your life, commit to a specific period of time, like thirty days, where you consciously apply these steps to your identified situation. Keep a journal to document your journey, noting your thoughts, emotions, beliefs, decisions, actions, and outcomes over this period. Adjust your approach based on the insights gained, and consider seeking coaching to uncover blind spots and refine your action plan.

By systematically applying the STEBDAR model, you not only gain insights into your thought processes and emotional responses but also empower yourself to take control of your actions and, ultimately, your life's direction. Remember, it's not what you see and then believe; it's believing so fiercely in your success that your brain makes it a reality. Are you ready to unlock your brain to believe in your extraordinary potential and turn those beliefs into reality?

Want to work with us to do this?

 Get started today at

67DAYYEARBOOK.COM

5

CLARIFY

The Power of Your 7 Whys

To help you crystallize this vision, I'll guide you through a quick exercise called the Power of 7 Whys. Once your brain has a crystal-clear picture, it will start working tirelessly to help you achieve it. This concept isn't new—it's been echoed in classics like *Think & Grow Rich*, and even in Scripture, which says, "As a man and a woman think, so shall they be" (Genesis 2:24).

This principle is at the heart of every incredibly successful person's journey. They all imprint their minds with such specific and vivid images of their success that failure becomes an impossibility. Daymond John himself shared that he woke up every morning and rewrote his vision in the present tense, as if it had already happened. Clients of mine have found similar success:

Lora joined the 67-Day Year because she wasn't seeing the monetary results she wanted. But she committed fully to the program and "trusting the process." When resistance arose, Lora would return to her vision and the Whys behind it. She created her first online course, acquired her first eleven paying customers, and moved the needle more in 67 days than she had in the previous three years combined.

Maari joined the 67-Day Year feeling stuck and burned out in her career as an artist and real estate investor. The work we did together helped her gain clarity on what she really wanted—and the Whys behind those desires—and how to move forward in a more sustainable, fulfilling way. Maari made significant progress on her goal of creating a new art style and developed a deeper understanding of her own thought patterns. We can achieve incredible things when we are crystal clear on why they matter to us.

Let's embark on this journey together. We're going to remove all fetters, all doubts, and dream again. We're going to Decide In Advance (DIA) what our future will hold. Remember, if you don't decide in advance, you're merely living out someone else's decisions. It's time to take control and shape the future you truly desire.

If you don't decide in advance, you're merely living out someone else's decisions.

WHAT DO YOU WANT?

The Power of 7 Whys helps uncover deeper motivations and align goals with core values, making it a powerful tool for personal transformation. We're not just aiming for a certain amount of money or a generic form of success. We're going to get specific. Imagine your ideal life as if you were living it now when you answer the questions below.

- What kind of body and health do you envision?
- What do your relationships with your spouse, kids, parents, and friends look like?
- What's your ideal environment?
- What work truly fulfills you?
- How are you spending your time, and with whom?
- What are you wearing, drinking, smelling, tasting, seeing, and hearing in all areas of your life?

This level of detail is crucial. Many people falter because they don't provide their brain with a vivid picture of their desired destination. Without this clarity, your brain can't effectively support your journey.

THE 7 WHYS EXERCISE

Now that you've envisioned your ideal life, it's time to explore the driving force behind your desires. We'll do this through a series of "Why" questions, each building on the previous one. This process uncovers the deeper motivations and gives substance to your aspirations.

- **Start with the first "Why":** Why do you want these things? Write down the first response that comes to mind.
- **Probe further:** Ask yourself, "Why does that reason matter?" Write down this answer.
- **Continue digging:** Keep asking "Why?" and writing down the responses until you have gone seven layers deep.

For example, my initial "Why" might be, "Because I want to make a difference in the world." As I probe further, I'll uncover that it's about contributing, impacting lives, modeling possibilities for my children, and ultimately fulfilling my purpose as a parent. This depth is what truly motivates and sustains our efforts, especially when challenges arise.

Once you have the first "Why," then ask yourself, "Why is that Why important?" Record that answer. Keep doing this until you have gone seven layers deep—in other words, 7 Whys.

FRAME YOUR DREAMS IN THE PRESENT TENSE

Now, take your dreams and frame them in the present tense, as if they're already realized. It's not about what you want, but what you've created. This shift in perspective trains your brain to believe in the reality of your dreams, making you an unstoppable force.

For example, instead of saying, "I want to start my own business," say, "I am the proud owner of a thriving business that allows me to make a significant impact in my community." This way, your brain begins to see your dreams as current realities, which aligns your actions and decisions with your goals.

Let's consider Maya, who dreams of opening her own bakery. We'll follow her through the 7 Whys to discover the deeper motivations behind her goal. This journey will also offer practical tips on conducting the 7 Whys exercise and address common challenges you might encounter along the way.

Initial Goal: Maya wants to open her own bakery.

Why do you want to open a bakery?

"Because I love baking and want to share my creations with the world."

Why do you love baking and want to share your creations?

"Because baking is my way of expressing love and creativity. Sharing my creations makes me feel connected to others."

Why is expressing love and creativity important to you?

"Because I grew up in a family where food was how we showed love, and being creative was always encouraged."

Why was food significant in showing love in your family?

"Because it brought us together, creating lasting memories and a sense of belonging."

Why are creating memories and a sense of belonging important?

"Because they make life meaningful. I want everyone who tries my baking to feel a part of something special."

Why do you want people to feel a part of something special?

"Because in today's busy world, moments of genuine connection are rare. I want my bakery to be a place where those moments happen."

Why are moments of genuine connection rare, and why do you want your bakery to facilitate them?

"Because people are often isolated and in a hurry. By creating a welcoming space, I can help bring joy and community back into their lives."

Through this exercise, Maya realizes her dream of opening a bakery isn't just about baking; it's deeply tied to her values of love, creativity, connection, and community.

Maya's story demonstrates the transformative power of understanding the deeper Whys behind our goals. By aligning her dream with her core values, Maya not only solidified her resolve but also mapped a path that resonates with her most profound beliefs. And she's not alone.

Tasha, a long-time client, made significant progress in removing negative beliefs that held her back. Her biggest win was stepping into her prime as a loving, confident, and joyful businesswoman, wife, mom, and friend who runs a wildly successful business with ease.

Embrace the process with openness, honesty, and patience. The 7 Whys exercise isn't just about uncovering the layers beneath your goals; it's about aligning your path with the essence of who you are, turning dreams into purpose-driven pursuits.

6

ERASE

The Mind Matrix

Ah, those pesky ANTs—automatic negative thoughts, often akin to what we know as limiting beliefs, truly act as the brain's brakes on our journey to success. Just like actual ants can invade a picnic and disrupt the peace, these mental ANTs invade our minds, creating doubts and fears that hinder our progress.

UNDERSTANDING AUTOMATIC NEGATIVE THOUGHTS (ANTS)

Automatic Negative Thoughts, or ANTs, are the little mental whispers that can stop us in our tracks. They're the limiting beliefs that tell us we're not smart enough, our dreams are too big, or we don't deserve success. These thoughts aren't random; they're rooted in past experiences, societal messages, and things we were taught growing up. They shape how we see ourselves and what's possible, keeping us stuck in familiar patterns.

To move past these ANTs, we need to recognize them for what they are: limiting beliefs. By identifying these thoughts, we can start to challenge and replace them with more empowering beliefs, effectively removing the mental brakes and accelerating toward our goals.

THE CHALLENGE OF OVERCOMING BRAIN BRAKES

You've got your goals set, you're full of energy, and you're repeating your goals every Monday, feeling sure you'll see your business skyrocket. But then, suddenly, you start feeling overwhelmed. Everything seemed perfect at first, but a few weeks later, you're stuck, helping others more than focusing on your own tasks. Your fast start begins to slow down, and you're left wondering, "Why is this happening? What should I do next?" This is what it feels like when those brain brakes hit.

Tackling these brain brakes means we need to look back at everything we've learned so far. It's time to really put STEBDAR and RADBETS into action, even more than before. Noticing these ANTs—those sneaky negative thoughts—isn't just a reminder of our journey toward reaching our goals; it also shows us how important it is to stay alert, keep pushing, and always work on thinking in a more positive way.

Now, we're at a critical point where we need to deal with these ANTs, kind of like calling in a brain bug exterminator. As we move ahead, we're going to focus even more on getting rid of those negative beliefs. We'll turn what could slow us down into chances to grow stronger and smarter. This step is all about using a cool strategy called the Mind Matrix, which is super important for making sure nothing blocks our way to success and happiness.

You learned earlier that your brain's primary job is to keep you safe and in familiar territory. Here's the not-so-great news: those limiting beliefs and old patterns, they're familiar territory. At some point, they were your brain's way of playing it safe. And because our education system doesn't teach us about these sneaky ants, they lie in wait, ready to disrupt your drive toward your goals and dreams.

WHY AFFIRMATIONS ALONE AREN'T ENOUGH

So why can't we bulldoze through these limiting beliefs with sheer willpower? Why don't affirmations alone cut it? You've probably guessed it by now: our brains thrive on automation, on repetition. Think of it in terms of physics: an object in motion stays in motion, and an object at rest stays at rest, unless an external force acts upon it. These limiting beliefs, these ingrained automations you didn't consciously choose—inherited from your family, your environment—they are that external force. Safe and familiar to your brain, but barriers to your aspirations.

Our brains thrive on automation, on repetition.

It's like you're in a car, foot on the accelerator, speeding toward your goals, filled with vision and momentum. But then, as the finite resource of willpower begins to wane—and let's face it, willpower is a neurochemical with a short shelf life of about two weeks—it's as though you suddenly slam your foot on the brake. That brake? It's your limiting beliefs. Now, picture this scenario—gas and brake pressed simultaneously. It's a struggle, a conflict within, where you're trying to move forward but are held back at the same time. This is the tussle of progressing with old, limiting automations at play.

And remember, these limiting beliefs—the automatic stories we never signed up for—are running 90 percent of our daily lives, influencing our decisions, actions, and ultimately our results.

So, how do we kick out these limiting beliefs? How do we erase a pathway from our brain so it stops spinning us out and slowing us down? We need something powerful, a tool to neutralize and erase these unwelcome guests from our mind.

Enter the Mind Matrix—four simple steps to obliterate a limiting belief. If there's one thing I hope you grasp at this point in the book, it's this: God designed it to be simple. Creating results and transformation? Simple. STEBDAR is a straightforward step-by-step path. Removing a limiting belief? Just as simple. So let's not waste any more time.

INTRODUCING THE MIND MATRIX

Imagine hitting a roadblock on the path to your goals, not because something's in your way but because your own brain keeps sending you in circles. Sounds frustrating, right? Well, that's exactly what happens when our subconscious is cluttered with negative thoughts and limiting beliefs. But there's good news: there's a way to clear these mental roadblocks, and it's called the Mind Matrix.

At the heart of the Mind Matrix lies a fascinating concept from neuroscience called synaptic pruning. Neuroscience has revealed that our brains are not static; they are dynamic and constantly changing. Synaptic pruning is the process by which the brain eliminates old, unnecessary connections between neurons, making room for new, more beneficial pathways. This natural process is the foundation of the Mind Matrix, offering us a powerful method to weed out thoughts and patterns that don't serve us and cultivate those that do. Think of your brain as a garden. Over time, some pathways (like garden paths) aren't used much and get overgrown, while we need to make new ones for better, quicker ways to get to our goals. Synaptic pruning is how your brain naturally tidies up, cutting out the old paths so you can build new, better ones.

The Mind Matrix isn't just a fancy trick; it's your brain's system for getting rid of those internal roadblocks. By following these steps, you're basically doing a spring cleaning for your brain, making sure it helps rather than hinders your journey to success. As we dive into the details of the Mind Matrix, remember that this tool is here to help you change your internal world so it matches the success you want to see in the real world. Let's get ready to roll up our sleeves and start gardening in our brains, paving the way to our dreams.

First, I'll outline these four steps right from the get-go, so you can see the simplicity for yourself. Then, we'll walk through each step together.

Step One: Recognize

The first step in the Mind Matrix is to recognize the limiting beliefs and automatic negative thoughts that are holding you back. This means becoming aware of the thoughts that repeatedly invade your mind and sabotage your progress. It's like turning on a light in a dark room—you can't fix what you can't see. Start by paying attention to your internal dialogue and identifying any recurring negative thoughts. Write them down. By recognizing and naming these thoughts, you take the first critical step toward dismantling them.

MIND MATRIX

1: Recognize

2: Record

3: Refute

4: Rewire

Step Two: Record

Once you've recognized these limiting beliefs, the next step is to record them. This involves documenting the specific negative thoughts and beliefs that you've identified. Keeping a journal can be incredibly helpful here. Write down each limiting belief in detail, noting when it occurs and how it makes you feel. Recording these thoughts externalizes them, making it easier to confront and address them. It's like creating a map of your mental landscape, highlighting the areas that need attention.

Step Three: Refute & Replace

With your limiting beliefs recorded, the third step is to refute them and replace them with more empowering beliefs. This involves challenging the validity of your negative thoughts. Ask yourself: Is this belief really true? What evidence do I have to support or refute it? Often, you'll find that these beliefs are based on assumptions or past experiences that no longer serve you. Once you've refuted the negative belief, replace it with a positive, empowering one. For example, if your limiting belief is "I'm not good enough," replace it with "I am capable and deserving of success."

Step Four: Rewire

The final step is to rewire your brain by consistently reinforcing the new, positive beliefs. This is where the power of repetition comes into play. Just as your brain formed the old pathways through repeated thoughts and experiences, it will form new ones through the same process. Use a tool called Truth Priming—a Brain Prime technique—to embed these new beliefs into your subconscious. Listen to your Truth Prime in the morning and evening, until these new thoughts become your default way of thinking. This step is about creating a new automatic response that aligns with your goals and aspirations.

PUTTING IT ALL TOGETHER

Yes, just four steps. If you can build with chunky LEGOs along-side a toddler, you can dismantle any brain brake or automatic negative thought that has ever dared to hold you back. So let's dive right into step one and start dismantling!

Understanding and implementing the Mind Matrix allows you to clear away the mental clutter that has been holding you back. By following these simple yet powerful steps, you can reprogram your mind to support your goals and dreams. Remember, creating lasting change is not about making drastic overnight transformations; it's about consistently applying these techniques to gradually reshape your thoughts and beliefs. As you move forward, keep in mind that every step you take brings you closer to a life by design, not by default. Let's get started on this journey of transformation, unlocking the full potential of your mind and paving the way to your dreams.

Every step you take brings you closer to a life by design, not by default.

STEP 1: RECOGNIZE IT

The first step in the Mind Matrix is all about recognition—understanding our unique human experiences and identifying the limiting beliefs that are holding us back. Each of us is unique, shaped by different paths, environments, and influences. This individuality means that the negative thoughts we experience, often labeled as impostor syndrome, are not "one size fits all." They manifest as thoughts like "Who will listen to me?" or "I can't believe anyone would care about what I have to say." These are rooted in fear—fear of being judged, fear of not being loved, fear of failure.

To truly recognize the limitations we've set for ourselves, we need to embrace our individuality and pay close attention to our internal dialogue. Think about what you're thinking about.

Think about what you're thinking about.

Recognize those moments when fear and doubt creep in. Again, these thoughts are not random; they're deeply ingrained beliefs formed from past experiences, societal messages, or things we were told growing up.

Embrace the Resistance

One effective way to tap into these limiting beliefs is to face resistance head-on. This means doing the things that scare you the most but are essential for your success. Whether it's going live on social media, pitching your product, or any other challenging task, these actions often trigger resistance. This resistance is your brain's way of trying to keep you safe in familiar territory.

When you hit resistance, it's often accompanied by physical sensations—tightness in your chest, butterflies in your stomach, a racing heartbeat. These are neurochemical responses to stepping out of your comfort zone. Recognizing these sensations helps you connect with the emotions tied to your subconscious thoughts.

Confronting Limiting Beliefs

Recognizing these thoughts is like detective work in your own mind. For example, when you decide to do something outside your comfort zone (like going live for the first time, giving a speech, or offering your services publicly), these actions can trigger your internal alarm system. By facing these challenges, you're able to tap into your subconscious and "hear" the thoughts that have been undermining your goals.

To put it simply, you need to know your enemy to defeat it. By recognizing these thoughts, you're taking the first crucial step toward neutralizing and erasing them. It's like shining a light in the dark corners of your mind and saying, "Aha! There you are!"

A Personal Example

When I started the *Epic Success* podcast, it was brand-new territory for me. Despite years of experience as a business consultant and coach, podcasting felt like a whole different ball game. My brain was not shy about reminding me of that, throwing up roadblocks at every turn.

But I felt a deep calling to share this message—to tell the world that you can indeed train your brain to transform your life and business. This mission felt like it came from God, especially knowing how many incredible people out there are held back from their true potential.

As I began the process of creating the podcast, I encountered resistance like never before. "What would I say? Who would listen to me?" These thoughts were relentless. But as I leaned into that discomfort, I finally heard the underlying thought clear as day: "I don't have enough value to bring to the podcast. Who would listen to me?"

That was the moment of recognition: Mind Matrix STEP 1. I was hearing, loud and clear, the self-doubt that my subconscious was whispering. It's like bringing something from the shadows into the light. By leaning into the resistance, by putting my brain in this bind, I was able to expose the limiting belief that was acting like a brake, slowing me down.

Leaning into Discomfort

Sitting down to record my first episode, I still felt those butterflies, but now I understood their source. The thought "I don't have enough value to bring to the podcast" had surfaced from the depths of my subconscious.

This part of the process is sensitive. It requires you to confront things you haven't confronted before, to push beyond familiar boundaries. And isn't that the very essence of growth?

Moving Forward

Once you've accomplished Step 1—recognition—you're ready for Step 2. Step 2 is where the transformation really begins to take shape. It's where we start to dismantle those limiting beliefs and pave the way for true growth. Recognizing and confronting these thoughts is the first crucial step in the journey to rewire your brain for success. Let's move forward with clarity and determination, embracing the process of transformation that the Mind Matrix offers.

STEP 2: RECORD IT

Once you've identified that pesky limiting thought, it's time to grab a pen and paper. Yes, the old-school way! Why? Because we're doing something powerful here—we're extracting these deep-seated automations from the hidden corners of our subconscious.

Think of your subconscious as a complex web, woven with memories, habits, and ingrained beliefs. Writing, with its tactile and motor skills, plays a crucial role in this process. It's like fishing out these thoughts and laying them bare on the page.

When I recognized my limiting belief ("I don't have enough value to bring to the podcast—who would listen to me?"), I didn't just think about it; I wrote it down. There's something almost magical about seeing your thoughts in your own handwriting. It makes them real, tangible, something you can actually tackle.

The Power of Writing

Writing by hand activates different parts of your brain compared to typing or thinking. The act of physically writing engages the brain in a unique way, helping to cement thoughts and make them more concrete. It forces you to slow down, process each word, and truly confront the belief you're dealing with.

Why This Step Is Crucial

Consider how many times you've tried to apply someone else's solutions—their affirmations, their "one size fits all" advice—to your unique, deeply personal wounds. It's like trying to put a band-aid on a broken arm. Our paths, our backgrounds, our experiences—they're all unique. And that's why we need a process that recognizes and respects our individuality.

Recording your limiting belief in your own handwriting allows you to:

- **Acknowledge Its Existence:** By writing it down, you're acknowledging the thought's presence in your mind. You're saying, "I see you. I recognize you're here."
- **Give It Form:** Putting it on paper gives it a physical form, making it something you can look at, analyze, and eventually confront.
- **Create a Starting Point:** This written record becomes your starting point for change. It's the "before" picture in your transformation journey.

A Personal Example

When I wrote down my limiting belief about the podcast, it felt like a weight lifted off my shoulders. The thought "I don't have enough value to bring to the podcast—who would listen to me?" was no longer this nebulous, intimidating presence in my mind. It was now a series of words on a piece of paper—words I could challenge and change.

By seeing this thought in my own handwriting, I could begin to dissect it, question its validity, and prepare to replace it with a more empowering belief. This act of writing it down was the bridge between recognizing the belief and actively working to change it.

The Steps in Action

To summarize, here's how you can put Step 2 into action:

- **Find a Quiet Space:** Choose a place where you won't be interrupted. This is your time to connect with your inner thoughts.
- **Use Pen and Paper:** Resist the temptation to type. The act of writing by hand is integral to this process.
- **Be Honest:** Write down the limiting belief exactly as it comes to you. Don't sugarcoat it or downplay it.
- **Reflect:** Take a moment to read what you've written. Acknowledge it without judgment. This is a part of your journey, and recognizing it is a crucial step forward.

Moving Forward

Now that you've recorded your limiting belief, you're ready for the next steps in the Mind Matrix. Step 1: Recognize it, where you bring the thought to light. Step 2: Record it, where you give your thought form and permanence. Next, we'll delve into how to challenge and replace these beliefs, setting the stage for true transformation.

By faithfully following this process, you're not just addressing surface-level issues; you're diving deep into the core of your subconscious mind, paving the way for profound and lasting change. Let's continue this journey with clarity and

You're diving deep into the core of your subconscious mind, paving the way for profound and lasting change.

confidence, knowing that each step brings us closer to unleashing our full potential.

STEP 3: REFUTE

This is where we channel our inner courtroom drama, just like I did sitting in awe of my uncle, the federal judge. Picture it: the courtroom's charged atmosphere, the suspenseful back-and-forth of arguments, the final, decisive verdict. That's exactly the energy we're bringing into refuting our limiting beliefs.

So, you've bravely leaned into resistance, felt every uncomfortable twist and turn, and let your brain put up a fight. You've navigated through the neurochemical storm—the butterflies, the nausea, the tension—and you've emerged with a crystal-clear recognition of your limiting belief. That's Step 1 nailed! Then, you've taken this elusive thought, made it tangible by writing it down in Step 2. You've dragged it out from the shadows of your subconscious into the stark light of day.

Now, it's time to play judge and jury. It's time to put this thought on trial in Step 3, Refute it. We're not just passively observing here; we're actively engaging. You're the judge, presiding over the case of *Your Limiting Belief vs. Your Potential Future.*

You're the judge, presiding over the case of Your Limiting Belief vs. Your Potential Future.

The thought you've uncovered? It's a lie. And in this step, you get to decide its fate. Does it stay, or does it go? If it's a thought that propels you toward your future, embrace it. But if it's a thought that's chaining you to the past, holding you back from your dreams and aspirations, then it's time to show it the door.

Refuting the lie in the Mind Matrix involves two critical components—the Logical and the Mirror. The Logical aspect is about dissecting the lie, understanding its falsity. It's about examining the evidence, just like in a courtroom, and seeing the thought for what it truly is—a barrier to your growth and success. The Mirror part is about addressing the emotions connected to this thought.

It's empowering, isn't it? You have the power to decide which thoughts serve your journey and which don't. You're not just a passive recipient of these automations; you're the director of your mind's narrative.

Logical Refute

Let's dive into the Logical Refute part of our journey. This is where we get a little *Law & Order*–style in our approach—think courtroom drama meets personal growth! You're the star prosecutor in the case against your limiting beliefs. So grab that pen and paper, and let's start building our case.

Imagine your limiting belief as the defendant, sitting nervously on the witness stand, about to face a barrage of truths. Your job? To marshal all the evidence that proves this belief is nothing but a big, fat lie. In my case, the lie was thinking I didn't have enough value to bring to my podcast. So I started jotting down every single piece of evidence to the contrary—from helping countless clients skyrocket their businesses to the value I've brought to my family. It was an avalanche of truth!

You'll do the same. Write down every single instance, big or small, that proves your limiting belief is just an illusion. The brain loves to solve puzzles, and this is one of the biggest puzzles of all—unraveling the lies we've told ourselves. By exploiting this "open loop" theory, you're actively rewiring your brain. It's like having a mental jackhammer at your disposal, breaking up the old, crumbly road of limiting beliefs to lay down a new pathway of empowering truths.

Here's the cool part: as you're listing down your evidence, your subconscious starts to get the message. It's like you've thrown it a curveball. It begins to question, "Wait, I thought we believed this? But all this evidence says otherwise!" Picture a construction site on a busy road, with workers tearing up the old asphalt. That's what you're doing to your old, limiting belief patterns.

So, you've now completed Step 1, Recognize it; Step 2, Record it; and Step 3, Refute it (logically). Remember, in our STEBDAR model, a belief is a combination of thought and emotion. We've just tackled the thought or logical component. But what about the emotion tied to that lie? That's what we're diving into next. We're not just going to dismantle the lie; we're going to strip away the emotional power it holds over us.

Alright, we've navigated the logical aspect of refuting those sneaky lies. Now, it's time for the Mirror step. This part is where things get personal and quite powerful. Trust me on this one; we're about to do some serious emotional hacking into our brain's subconscious.

Mirror or Emotional Refute

Step one of the Mirror involves picking your ride-or-die—that person you'd do absolutely anything for. It could be your spouse, one of your kids, or a dear friend. I know it's tough to pick just one, but let's focus here. Remember, this is about evoking strong emotional responses, so choose the person who means the world to you.

Once you've got your ride-or-die in mind, the second step is a bit more sensitive. You're going to take that lie you've been wrestling with and imagine a bully is saying it out loud to your chosen person. But wait—you're not actually going to say it to them. This exercise is done privately, where you're safe to express these thoughts without any real-world implications.

For example, I chose my son, Max. In a room by myself, I verbalized the lie to him. Out loud I repeated what the bully said (the lie): "Max, you don't have enough value to bring to the world. No one will listen to you." It felt wrong even just saying it to the air, but that's the point.

Next comes the real magic—step three. It's time to become your loved one's fiercest advocate. Picture yourself as a protective lioness or a warrior. You're going to passionately counter that lie as if someone dared to say it to your ride-or-die. Get ready to put on those metaphorical boxing gloves and fight back.

Passionately counter that lie as if someone dared to say it to your ride-or-die.

Here's what it looked like for me: "Are you kidding me? Max is incredible! He's intelligent and caring; he makes a significant impact on everyone he meets. Of course people will listen to him—he's going to change the world with his passion and kindness!"

Feel the intensity? This exercise pulls out deep emotions because, let's face it, we would never tolerate anyone else speaking such lies over our loved ones. It's a powerful reflection, isn't it? It shows us how fiercely we should defend ourselves against these limiting beliefs. Because if we wouldn't accept them for our ride-or-die, why on Earth should we accept them for ourselves?

This part of the Mind Matrix often brings up strong feelings, and that's okay. It's part of the healing and transformative process. By defending your ride-or-die against these lies, you're simultaneously breaking down the emotional stronghold of your own limiting beliefs. It's an emotional but incredibly effective way to shatter those barriers.

Everything you passionately defended for your ride-or-die—guess what? That's the truth about you, too! But it's been hidden under layers of self-doubt and negativity bias. That's right, science has shown us that we're wired to see ourselves in a harsher, more negative light compared to how we view others. It's like having a skewed mirror that only reflects back the negatives about ourselves, magnifying them almost ninefold!

So, when you bravely spoke out those lies about your loved one and vehemently defended them, you were actually revealing the truths about yourself that you were just unable to recognize. This is a powerful moment of realization. You've been carrying these burdensome lies for years, maybe decades, shaping your decisions and actions under their heavy weight. Yet the moment you externalize them onto someone you care deeply about, your true feelings and beliefs come roaring to the surface, ready to defend and protect.

Now, here's the crucial step in the Mirror phase of the Mind Matrix—take every single thing you've written in defense of your loved one and rephrase it in the first person. Yes, personalize it, because if it's true for them, it's undeniably true for you. And here's the kicker—most of what you'll write down will be emotionally charged, vibrant, and full of life. This isn't just an exercise; it's a powerful tool that accelerates the process of shattering those limiting beliefs. Don't skip this part. It's the fuel that will propel you forward in this journey of transformation.

Now, I know what you're thinking. "Shannon, I must have a million of these limiting beliefs. This is going to be a marathon!" But let me share a little secret: Most of our beliefs boil down to a few core questions: "Am I safe? Am I loved? Do I have value?" When we tackle these head on, it's like pulling a thread that unravels the entire tapestry of falsehoods that have held us back.

With the third step complete, we are now ready to move to the final phase of the Mind Matrix: Rewire. This next step will consolidate all the work you've done so far, ensuring that the new beliefs are deeply embedded into your psyche, setting you firmly on the path to achieving your true potential.

STEP 4: REWIRE

This is where the real change takes root. Up until now, you've identified the lie, gathered evidence against it, and emotionally refuted it. You're standing on the precipice of freedom, armed with truth.

Picture the scene: on your desk lies a compilation of truths, a testament to your inner strength and resilience. These truths are your liberation, echoing the scripture, "the truth shall set you free." But we're not just stopping at recognizing the truth. We're about to engrave it into our minds, creating a superhighway that leads directly to it.

This is where Brain Prime comes into play, specifically the Truth Prime method. Through this process, we're not just making it difficult to traverse the old, destructive pathways of lies and limitations. We're obliterating them. This isn't just roadwork; it's a complete demolition and reconstruction. The freeway of falsehoods that once guided your thoughts and actions? It's going to vanish, replaced by a clear, unobstructed path to your new truth.

Imagine this: the lies that once controlled your life are now mere rubble, unable to support any traffic of thoughts or actions. In their place, a wide, open road emerges, leading you toward the truth you've acknowledged and embraced. This new pathway isn't just a small trail; it's a major freeway, designed for high-speed travel toward your goals, dreams, and true potential.

Through the Truth Prime, we're solidifying this new path. It's not enough to just acknowledge the truth—we need to embed it into our subconscious. This means repetition, reinforcement, and unwavering commitment. Every time you reinforce this truth, the pathway becomes more robust, more permanent. It's like laying down layer after layer of smooth, solid asphalt, making it the preferred route for your thoughts and actions.

It's not enough to just acknowledge the truth—we need to embed it into our subconscious.

But remember, this isn't a one-time effort. The brain loves repetition—it's how it learns best. So, by continuously engaging in the Truth Prime process, you're ensuring that this new, empowering path becomes your brain's go-to route, your new autopilot setting. This is how lasting transformation happens. Not overnight, but through consistent, deliberate practice.

7

Reticular Activation System

Alright, let's dive deeper and speed up! We've discovered that if we're not careful, our brains can run on autopilot, letting old habits shape what we do now and in the future. Now, I want to introduce you to something amazing in our brains called the reticular activating system, or RAS for short.

Tony Robbins, a well-known motivational speaker, really brought the RAS into the spotlight. He would do these eye-opening exercises at his big events where he'd tell everyone to try not to notice anything red in the room. Well, guess what happened next? Suddenly, all anyone could see was the color red everywhere. This is a perfect example of the RAS at work.

UNDERSTANDING THE RAS:
YOUR BRAIN'S BOUNCER

Picture the RAS as a super strong guard who watches over the entrance to your subconscious mind—a big, alert bouncer who's about 6'5" tall, standing firm at the door of your mind's inner world. This guard's job is to decide what gets to come into your conscious awareness.

Now let's break down how this mental "bouncer" does its job, especially when it comes to sorting through information that matches or doesn't match our deep-down beliefs. The RAS has this incredible ability to filter out tons of information we come across every day. It helps us focus on things that matter to us based on our beliefs and what we think is important.

For example, if you believe that being kind is super important, your RAS will help you notice acts of kindness around you more often. Or if you're really into basketball, it's like your RAS puts on a pair of basketball goggles—you'll start to see basketball-related stuff everywhere, from noticing more games on TV to spotting basketball courts as you walk around your neighborhood.

HOW THE RAS FILTERS INFORMATION
BASED ON YOUR BELIEFS

What's really happening is that the RAS filters the information that comes our way, letting through only the stuff that lines up with our beliefs or what we focus on. It's like the RAS is constantly asking, "Hey, is this piece of information important to us? Does it match what we already believe?" If the answer is yes, it lets it through to our conscious mind, making us pay attention to it.

Understanding the RAS can be a game changer. Once you know how it works, you can start to train this mental bouncer by shifting your focus or changing your beliefs. This way, you can start noticing and attracting more of what you want into your life, whether that's positivity, opportunities, or even just spotting more of your favorite color.

Start noticing and attracting more of what you want into your life.

Instead, our brain follows a set of prewritten scripts, replaying the ones we've practiced the most, many of which got their start when we were kids. If we haven't yet started reprogramming those old scripts through methods like transformative coaching or deliberate self-improvement, we might find ourselves stuck in old patterns that don't really match where we want to go now.

This is why it's so important to take active steps toward rewriting these old scripts. It highlights the need for being mindful, setting clear intentions, and using specific strategies for personal growth. By doing this, we can truly tap into the power of our minds and steer our lives in the direction we truly want to go.

Imagine growing up in an environment where you were constantly told that "Money is the root of all evil" or that those who are wealthy gained their fortune through exploitation. Perhaps this message was reinforced in your family or even in your church, painting a picture of virtue in poverty. It's important to clarify, though, that the original scripture actually points to the love of money, rather than money itself, as the root of evil. But let's say this belief about money was deeply ingrained in you.

Now picture yourself as an entrepreneur, aiming to make a difference, yet carrying the belief that "money is evil." In such a scenario, your RAS acts like a strict bouncer, refusing entry to any thought, opportunity, or perspective that doesn't align with this deep-rooted belief. So what do you think happens when you're trying to sell a product or grow a business? Your RAS effectively blinds you to possibilities and opportunities that conflict with this belief. This selective awareness, governed by the RAS, can prevent you from recognizing or even considering avenues that could lead to financial success.

SHERI'S STORY: OVERCOMING LIMITING BELIEFS ABOUT MONEY

Sheri is one of my brilliant clients in the 67-Day Year coaching program. Sheri had this ingrained belief that making money was an uphill battle, almost a herculean task. Picture being in a relationship where you've convinced yourself the other person is nothing but trouble, even if they're not. That was Sheri with money—she perceived it as a source of difficulty, almost villainous. You can imagine how this belief skewed her relationship with financial success. She was amazing at what she did, always going above and beyond, but when it came to asking for payment, she'd shy away, believing a "good person" shouldn't be so forward. And social media? Out of the question for her—too egocentric for her taste.

When Sheri joined my 67-Day Year coaching program, we were able to pinpoint the subconscious beliefs standing in her way. She realized her negative thoughts about money, like feeling wrong to ask for payment or thinking it's show-offy to promote her work, were based on a deep belief that "money is bad." She could see how these beliefs had made her feel guilty and scared about money, which made it really hard for her to get what she deserved for her amazing work.

But here's the twist—these beliefs about money weren't even truly hers; they were just the old tapes playing in her head, her subconscious's autopilot mode. It was like driving with one foot on the brake and the other on the gas—getting nowhere fast. Once she saw how this belief was holding her back, Sheri decided it was time to see things differently.

In our program, Sheri embraced the STEBDAR method and mastered the Mind Matrix, a tool for dismantling and rebuilding mental scripts. She tackled those deep-seated beliefs about money head-on, replacing them with empowering new ones. Through the Brain Prime system, she rewired her subconscious to align with her true aspirations.

The transformation was nothing short of miraculous. In just four weeks, she leapt from zero sales to a staggering $110,000, attracting twelve incredible clients. Sheri's transformation wasn't about a new strategy or some marketing gimmick. Sheri changed the narrative in her mind. She turned on her brain's success switch, and suddenly, her mental doorman, the RAS, swung the doors wide open to opportunities she'd been blind to before.

PROGRAMMING YOUR BRAIN FOR SUCCESS

The brain is simpler than we think. It automates what we repeat. So now our mission is to change what's in automation. We're not just tweaking a few thoughts here and there; we're reprogramming the command center of our lives. God has given us an incredible gift in our brain. It's up to us to use it wisely, to align it with His promises and the greatness He has in store for us.

> God has given us an incredible gift in our brain. It's up to us to use it wisely.

Understanding the power of the reticular activating system (RAS) has opened our eyes to the brain's remarkable ability to focus on what we deem important. It's clear now that our brains operate on patterns we repeatedly enforce, whether consciously or not. This realization brings us to an essential turning point: It's time to actively reprogram our brain's automated responses to ensure they align with the success and fulfillment we seek.

Recognizing the gift of our brain, we must commit to using this gift to its fullest potential, directing it toward the positive, the hopeful, and the divine promises meant for our lives. As we stand on the brink of this transformative journey, our immediate next step is clear: We must prepare to engage with a powerful tool known as the Brain Prime.

The Brain Prime technique is your key to unlocking this new phase of success. As we transition into the next chapter, I urge you to focus on how you can train your brain to not only recognize success but to welcome and achieve it. The Brain Prime will provide you with practical steps to adjust your RAS, helping you to filter in opportunities, positivity, and the potential for growth that you might have been previously conditioned to overlook.

Let's move forward with intention and faith, ready to take control of our brain's programming. By doing so, we align ourselves not just with our personal aspirations but also with the higher purpose we are called to fulfill. The journey ahead is one of transformation, discovery, and unprecedented success, starting with mastering the Brain Prime to rewire our minds for the success we truly deserve.

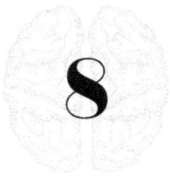

8

AUTOMATE

Brain Prime

Brain Prime is a method that prepares your brain to recognize, focus on, and pursue the things you really want in life. It's about setting up your mind in a way that automatically aligns your thoughts and actions with your deepest desires.

The Brain Prime system works by repeatedly exposing your mind to specific ideas, goals, or attitudes until they become second nature. Just like programming a computer to perform certain tasks automatically, Brain Priming programs your mind to subconsciously seek out and engage with opportunities that match your ambitions.

Here's how it connects to automating your desires: By consistently focusing on positive and goal-oriented thoughts, your brain starts to prioritize these thoughts over others. This means you'll naturally start to take actions that bring you closer to your goals, almost without having to think about it consciously. It's like setting a cruise control for success based on the destination you've programmed into your brain's GPS.

To kickstart this process, we'll dive into specific strategies and exercises designed to prime your brain. This isn't just wishful thinking; it's about actively shaping your thought patterns to create a powerful, automatic drive toward achieving what matters most to you.

It's about making a conscious choice every day about what you're going to serve.

It's about making a conscious choice every day about what you're going to serve. See, in our world, when you grasp the process, the path becomes clear. The brain's transformation for success and results involves seven steps, but honestly, it can be distilled down to three essential elements. And at its core, it's about what you keep repeating.

It's astonishingly simple, yet so many of us miss it, getting lost in the pursuit of external strategies and tactics. Why? Because we've been conditioned to believe that the answers lie outside of us. We've been taught to seek validation, to wait for permission, to rely on someone else's intelligence. This "outside-in" philosophy, deeply ingrained since our school days, tells us success is about grades, about pleasing others.

THE SCIENCE BEHIND BRAIN PRIME

Brain Priming is supported by neuropsychology, which studies how the brain's structure and functions relate to behavior and cognition. The concept of Brain Priming aligns with the understanding that repeated exposure to certain stimuli strengthens neural pathways, making the associated thoughts, actions, or feelings more automatic. This is due to neuroplasticity, the brain's ability to change and adapt over time. When you focus consistently on specific goals or attitudes, you're leveraging this adaptability to rewire your brain toward those objectives, enhancing your ability to recognize and seize opportunities that align with your desires.

Understanding Brain Priming and its support from neuropsychology is like unlocking a secret level in a video game—it gives you an edge in achieving your dreams. Neuropsychology tells us that our brain changes based on our experiences, thoughts, and actions. This is called neuroplasticity. When you focus again and again on specific goals or attitudes, you're tapping into this incredible ability. You're rewiring your brain to spot and grab the opportunities that can make your dreams come true.

CRAFTING YOUR BRAIN PRIME

Step 1: Visualize Your Goals

First, find a quiet spot where you can really think. Decide what you want more than anything. Picture it in your mind, but don't just see it—feel it. Imagine your goal with all the color, emotion, and energy you can muster. For instance, say to yourself, "I'm standing in front of a crowd, sharing my ideas confidently. Everyone is listening, nodding, and smiling. I'm making a difference with my work, and it fills me with a deep sense of joy and purpose." Continue until every desire for your Epic Audacious

Goals are written down. It should feel like a script of a movie that is already showing the results and what you write down should be in the language of the present tense, not future tense—as if it has already happened.

Step 2: Connect with Your Why

Then dig into why this dream lights a fire in you. What makes it so important? Connect your goal to your heart. "This dream matters because I want to leave a mark, to show the world that one person's creativity can change lives for the better. I want to look back on my life and know I lived fully, with purpose and passion."

Step 3: Record Your Vision

Now take this vivid, emotionally charged vision and record yourself reading all the things that you wrote down—in the present tense as if it has already happened. Use a voice that's brimming with confidence and happiness.

EXERCISE TO CREATE
YOUR BRAIN PRIME

Listen Every Day: Play your recording every night before you sleep—this is when your brain is getting ready for the next day. Listen again in the morning to set your brain's focus on making your goal a reality.

Visualize Like a Pro: Dedicate 5–10 minutes every day to close your eyes and immerse yourself in your success. See every detail, feel every emotion as if you're living your dream at that moment.

Take Action with Journaling: After visualizing, jot down three steps you can take today to move closer to your goal. Keep an eye out for any new opportunities or ideas that come up since you've started your Brain Prime.

By embracing this Vision Brain Prime routine, you're not just wishing for success; you're programming your brain to lead you there. It's about turning your subconscious into your biggest ally, making the path to your dreams not just possible but inevitable. Let's harness the power of Brain Prime to transform our lives, making every day a step closer to where we want to be. Remember, your brain is a powerhouse waiting for your command—guide it with purpose, passion, and persistence.

BRAIN PRIMING

1: Visualize

2: Connect

3: Record

RADBETS: HACKING SUCCESS FROM THE INSIDE OUT

It is crucial to understand that success isn't just about the external accolades or meeting someone else's standards. It's about what you feed your mind and how that shapes everything you do. We often get caught up looking for answers and approval from the world around us, thinking success comes from external achievements. However, the real journey to success starts from within.

This brings us to RADBETS, a clever way to remember the internal steps toward transforming your mind for success. It stands for:

Results	The outcomes you desire.
Actions	The steps you need to take.
Decisions	The choices that lead to action.
Beliefs	The underlying convictions that drive decisions.
Emotions	The feelings that fuel beliefs.
Thoughts	The mental dialogues that shape emotions.
Situations	The external circumstances influenced by internal states.

This should feel familiar—as it is reverse engineering STEBDAR. STEBDAR is how the brain creates a subconscious pattern. RADBETS is how we hack or hijack that system to speed up results! It also helps us uncover any blind spots that may be in the way.

This reverse acronym reminds us to start with our inner world—our desires, beliefs, and thoughts—allowing them to inform our actions and decisions. It's about shifting from seeking validation from the outside to cultivating strength and direction from the inside.

So, as we dive deeper into this journey, remember: the key to unlocking your full potential lies not in chasing external benchmarks, but in harnessing the power of your mind through Brain Prime and embracing the RADBETS approach to foster internal growth and transformation.

UNDERSTANDING THE SHIFT: FROM EXTERNAL TO INTERNAL VALIDATION

In our journey through life, we often find ourselves at a crossroads, faced with the choice of seeking approval from the world around us or turning inward to find validation from within. This choice shapes not just the decisions we make but the very essence of who we become. To truly grasp the significance of shifting from external to internal validation, it's crucial to understand the traditional framework that prioritizes the external.

The Traditional External Focus

Traditionally, society teaches us to measure our worth and success through external benchmarks. From a young age, we're conditioned to seek approval and recognition from others, whether it's through grades in school, accolades in our careers, or likes on social media. This external focus is deeply ingrained in our culture, guiding us to value what others think of us above all.

> **Grades and Academic Achievement:** From the moment we enter the education system, we're taught that our intellectual value is tied to the grades we receive, fostering a reliance on external validation for our academic endeavors.

Career Success: In the professional realm, promotions, titles, and accolades become the yardsticks by which we measure our worth, often leading us to pursue paths more aligned with societal expectations than our own passions.

Social Approval: The advent of social media has amplified the need for external validation, with likes, shares, and followers becoming significant markers of social worth and acceptance.

This external focus creates a dependency on the approval of others, making our self-esteem and sense of achievement contingent on factors outside our control. It sets us on a path where our happiness and fulfillment are perpetually at the mercy of the changing opinions and standards of the world around us.

The Internal Mindset Shift

The turning point comes when we realize that true fulfillment and lasting success cannot be found in external validation. This realization marks the beginning of a profound internal shift toward seeking validation from within.

Self-Awareness: The first step is becoming aware of our inherent worth, independent of external achievements. This involves recognizing our unique talents, values, and passions.

Self-Belief: Building a strong belief in our abilities and potential, regardless of external feedback, is crucial. This belief empowers us to pursue our goals with confidence and resilience.

Self-Validation: Learning to validate ourselves for our efforts and progress, rather than the outcome, fosters a sense of internal satisfaction that is not reliant on external recognition.

Purpose-Driven Action: With a focus on internal validation, our actions become aligned with our true selves and purpose, leading to more authentic and fulfilling life choices.

By understanding the traditional framework that emphasizes external validation, we can more fully appreciate the transformative power of shifting our focus inward. This internal mindset shift not only liberates us from the confines of societal expectations but also opens the door to a more authentic, purposeful, and satisfying life. As we navigate this shift, we equip ourselves with the tools to build a foundation of self-worth that is unwavering in the face of external change, setting the stage for genuine success and happiness.

But remember: to flip this script, you've got to reverse it—RADBETS, the reverse acronym of the steps your brain takes for transformation. Instead of waiting for external validation, you start with internal transformation. You start with what you repeat, what you believe, and let that shape your actions and decisions. It's a complete mindset overhaul, moving from seeking external approval to fostering internal growth.

Instead of waiting for external validation, you start with internal transformation.

101

If you want different results, you've got to embrace different actions. It's like changing gears in a car; to accelerate, you can't stick to the same gear. And to shift your actions, you first need to shift your decisions. But here's the catch: your decisions are rooted in your beliefs. And these beliefs? They sprout from the seeds of your thoughts, nourished by your emotions. So, to alter your beliefs, you've got to start with changing your thoughts and feelings. No more waiting for external cues—it's time to take control from the inside out.

> *If you want different results, you've got to embrace different actions.*

OVERCOMING LIMITING BELIEFS

Let's circle back to the story of my competitive friend. Remember the one I raced to the finish line without a governor on my golf cart? The only thing separating us was that tiny piece of hardware—she had a governor, and I didn't. This is a perfect metaphor for what we're tackling next: those pesky limiting beliefs, the invisible governors in our minds. They're like having your foot on the gas, racing toward your goals, but unbeknownst to you, there's a hidden brake being pressed simultaneously. These limiting beliefs are subtly aligning your actions not with who you aim to be but with who you've always been. They're the roadblocks to your desired destination.

In the next chapter, we're going to dissect these limiting beliefs and then, more importantly, I'll show you how to dismantle them in four straightforward steps. It's time to release that brake, remove the governor, and let your potential soar unbounded. We're not just learning brain science here; we're aligning with a divine blueprint for success.

9

Truth Brain Prime

As we apply the Mind Matrix, we arrive at an enlightening stage: the Truth Brain Prime. This is where simplicity and profundity intertwine, where the straightforward act of embracing truth has the power to shift mountains in our minds.

Why is embracing the truth crucial for personal growth? When we dive into the Mind Matrix, hitting the Truth Brain Prime stage is like turning on a bright light in a dark room for your brain's networks. This is the step where we prune away the old, broken neural networks that have been running our dreams into the ground. This is where everything gets real simple but also super deep. It's all about understanding how accepting the real truth about ourselves can seriously change our lives for the better.

Getting real with the truth about who we are, what we can do, and what we dream of is super important for growing as a person. Think of the truth as a mirror showing us everything—the good stuff and the stuff we might not be so proud of. It cuts through the excuses and the doubts that hold us back. Knowing and facing the real you lays down the strongest foundation for making big changes in your life.

The truth is powerful. It's like the ground we stand on. It's what helps us build a life that feels right and stands strong, even when things get tough. Accepting the truth about ourselves asks us to be brave and honest, but it also sets us free to reach for more.

Once we start embracing the Truth Prime, we're basically giving ourselves a green light to grow and achieve our dreams. It's like finally getting a clear map to a treasure we've been searching for. With the truth, what seemed impossible starts to look doable. Our goals get bigger, we dare to step out of our comfort zones, and we start seeing challenges as chances to shine.

Once we start embracing the Truth Prime, we're basically giving ourselves a green light to grow and achieve our dreams.

The truth is transformational because it flips how we see ourselves and the world around us. Instead of being our own toughest critics, we become our biggest supporters. This doesn't just help us internally; it changes how we act, making us more likely to take on new opportunities and chase our dreams with confidence.

Accepting the truth isn't just something you do once and then forget about. It's a journey that keeps going as we grow and change. It's easy to slip back into old ways of thinking, so we need to stay sharp and keep reminding ourselves of our truths. The Truth Prime teaches us to keep checking in with ourselves, to keep our truths updated, and to stay true to our path.

In short, the Truth Brain Prime shines a spotlight on how important it is to be honest with ourselves. It's about being true, staying strong in who we are, and using that strength to live out our biggest dreams. By sticking to our truths, we're not just making our lives better—we're also inspiring others to start their own journey of growth and discovery. That's the real magic of embracing the truth: it opens up a world of possibilities and helps us live our best lives.

SARAH'S STORY

Let's talk about Sarah, a 35-year-old woman who had big dreams but was also full of self-doubt. Sarah dreamed of opening her own café, a place that would be more than just somewhere to get coffee—it would be a community hub, full of warmth and friendship. However, despite her passion and detailed plans, Sarah was stuck. Her mind was filled with negative thoughts like, "I'm too old to start something new," "I probably don't have the right skills," and "What if I fail?" These worries kept her from making her dream a reality.

Then one evening, Sarah came across a Bible verse that really hit home: Philippians 4:13, "I can do all things through Christ who strengthens me." This verse was a breakthrough for her. It made her think differently and want to change her mindset. She remembered learning about something called the Mind Matrix and the Truth Prime technique, which gave her an idea.

Sarah started by listing all the negative thoughts that were holding her back. She then created positive statements to counteract these thoughts, like "God has given me everything I need to succeed," "My age gives me wisdom and experience," and "Every mistake is just a step closer to success."

Next, Sarah recorded these positive statements in her own voice, making an audio track called her Truth Prime. She listened to this recording every morning when she woke up and every night before going to bed. This practice began to change the way she thought about herself and her dream.

Gradually, Sarah started to feel different. She became more confident and started taking action toward her goal. She signed up for business classes, sought advice from people who knew about running a café, and finally took the big step of renting a space for her café.

The day her café opened was a big victory. It wasn't just about serving great coffee; it was proof that she had overcome her fears and doubts. Her café became exactly what she'd hoped—a place where people came together, and community grew. It was a dream come true, all because she chose to train her brain, to believe in herself and trust in God's plan for her.

Sarah's story is a perfect example of what the Bible means when it says in Romans 12:2: "Do not conform to the pattern of this world, but be transformed by the renewing of your mind." It shows us that when we fill our minds with positive, Godly truths, we can break through the barriers of doubt and fear. By using the Truth Prime and leaning on faith, Sarah didn't just achieve her dream; she stepped into the life God had planned for her. Her journey is a powerful reminder that with faith, the right mindset, and action, we can conquer our fears and live out our dreams.

IMPLEMENTING YOUR TRUTH PRIME

You've already traversed the initial steps of the Mind Matrix—recognizing and recording your limiting beliefs, and then robustly refuting them, both logically and emotionally. Now, with your newfound truths articulated in the first person, it's time to transform these truths into an unstoppable force within your mind. Don't skip this step unless you want the limiting beliefs to stay 90 percent in control of your future and results in this world—and I know you don't want that!

Creating and using a Truth Brain Prime audio recording, in addition to the Vision Brain Prime, is a powerful way to transform your mindset and propel you toward your goals. Here's a detailed, step-by-step guide to help you craft and effectively use your own Truth Prime, starting with the 4 Rs of the Mind Matrix:

Step 1: Identify Your Limiting Beliefs

Recognize: Spend some time reflecting on the negative thoughts that frequently cross your mind. These could be about your abilities, your worth, or your potential.

Record: Make a list of these limiting beliefs. Be honest and thorough.

Step 2: Reframe Into Empowering Truths

Refute—Counteract Each Belief: For every limiting belief you've listed, write an empowering statement that contradicts it. This should reflect a truth about your abilities, your worth, and your potential that you want to reinforce. Use both the Logical and the Mirror techniques from the Mind Matrix chapter.

Replace—First Person and Present Tense: Phrase these statements in the first person and present tense to make them more powerful and personal (e.g., "I am capable of achieving my goals").

Step 3: Prepare to Record

Quiet Space: Find a quiet, comfortable space where you won't be interrupted.

Good Quality Recording Device: This can be a smartphone or a computer with a microphone. Make sure the recording quality is clear.

Step 4: Record Your Truth Prime—REWIRE!

Relaxed and Confident Tone: Speak in a calm, confident tone. Your future self is listening.

Emotion and Belief: Try to infuse each statement with emotion and belief, even if it feels challenging at first. The more you believe in what you're saying, the more effective the recording will be. Describe it like you were seeing it as a movie and it has already happened!

Step 5: Incorporate Brain Prime
into Your Daily Routine

Morning Routine: Listen to your Vision Brain Prime and Truth Prime recording first thing in the morning. This sets a positive tone for your day and focuses your mind on your truths.

Night Routine: Listen again before you go to bed. This allows your subconscious to process these truths overnight.

Consistency Is Key: Make this practice a nonnegotiable part of your daily routine. For a more immersive experience, listen with headphones. This can help minimize distractions and make the message more impactful.

As you grow and evolve, so will your truths. Update your recording periodically to reflect new beliefs and goals. Combining auditory and visual cues can enhance the impact, so you may want to try combining it with visualization. While listening, try to visualize yourself living out these truths.

BRINGING IT ALL TOGETHER

When you create your Truth Brain Prime recording, you're not just speaking words—you're laying the foundation for a new, empowered mindset. This practice, rooted in both scientific understanding of brain plasticity and the transformative power of faith, can help you break free from the limitations of the past and step boldly into the future God has planned for you. By consistently reinforcing these truths, you're training your brain to embrace them fully, making them an integral part of your daily life.

Remember, this is a journey. Just as Romans 12:2 reminds us to be transformed by the renewing of our minds, your daily commitment to the Truth Brain Prime will help you continually renew and strengthen your mindset, aligning it with your deepest truths and highest aspirations.

When you start working on embracing your truths, especially using something like the Truth Prime audio recordings, it's like you're setting off on a big adventure to discover the real you. But just like any adventure, there are going to be some challenges along the way. Let's look at what some of these might be and how you can jump over these hurdles, backed by science and faith.

You're setting off on a big adventure to discover the real you.

If You Feel Silly or Skeptical: It's normal to feel a bit awkward or skeptical at first. Keep an open mind and give it time. The more you listen, the more natural it will feel.

If You're Feeling Doubtful: It might feel a bit strange or doubtful to say good things about yourself, especially if you're used to thinking the opposite. You might wonder if just listening to positive statements can really change anything.

Science shows us through studies on neuroplasticity—that's a fancy way of saying our brains can change and adapt—that repeating positive affirmations can actually rewire our brains. Plus, the Bible tells us in Romans 12:2 about being transformed by the renewal of our mind. So, when you're embracing your truths, you're on the right track scientifically and spiritually. Keep going, and trust the process.

If You're Struggling to Find Your True Beliefs: The challenge is that sometimes it's hard to figure out what you truly believe about yourself. You might not even realize you have certain negative beliefs holding you back.

Start by reflecting on areas of your life where you feel stuck or unhappy. What negative thoughts pop up? Flip those into positive statements for your Truth Prime. Remember, discovering these truths is a journey—like digging for hidden treasure. Pray for guidance and clarity as you do this, trusting that God will reveal the deep truths within you.

If You're Struggling to Stick to It Every Day: Life gets busy, and it can be hard to listen to your Truth Prime recordings regularly. Treat this time like it's as important as eating or sleeping. It's nourishment for your mind. Set reminders on your phone or put it in your schedule as a daily appointment with yourself. Remember, consistency is key to letting those truths sink in and start transforming your thoughts.

If It's Hard Dealing with Emotional Ups and Downs: Some days, you might feel overwhelmed by negative emotions, making it tough to believe the positive truths you're trying to embrace. It's okay to have tough days. During these times, focus on truths that remind you of God's love and strength within you, like "I am loved by God, even on my hardest days." Science shows us that acknowledging our emotions and then deliberately focusing on positive affirmations can help lift our mood and mindset.

If You're Fighting Off the Negative Thoughts: Even as you work on embracing positive truths, negative thoughts might still creep in, trying to throw you off course. Picture your mind like a garden. You're the gardener, choosing what gets to grow. When negative thoughts appear, acknowledge them, then consciously choose to focus on your positive Truth Prime instead. Remember, Philippians 4:8 tells us to think about whatever is true, noble, right, pure, lovely, and admirable. This is your spiritual and mental gardening guide.

By following these steps and tips, you create not just an audio recording but a personalized tool for mental transformation. The Truth Brain Prime is your ally in the journey toward a more positive, empowered mindset, laying the foundation for achieving your deepest aspirations.

MOVING FORWARD WITH
SCIENCE AND FAITH

As you face these challenges, remember that what you're doing is supported by both science and scripture. By actively choosing to embrace and repeat God's truths about you, you're not just changing your brain on a physical level; you're also stepping into the identity God has for you. This journey of embracing your truths is a powerful way God renews and transforms your mind, helping you grow into the person He designed you to be. Keep pushing through the challenges, and watch how your adventure unfolds into something beautiful.

In addition to the Truth Brain Prime, there's also the Vision Brain Prime—a topic we'll explore in depth in the coming chapter. Together, these primes form a powerful duo, guiding your subconscious toward a future aligned with your highest aspirations.

THE CONNECTION BETWEEN THE
TRUTH PRIME AND THE MIND MATRIX

Let's dive deeper into how the Truth Prime connects with the rest of the Mind Matrix and why this combo is super powerful for changing your life. Think of the Mind Matrix as a team where each player has a special role, but they all work together to win the game. The Truth Brain Prime is like the star player that scores the goals, but it needs the rest of the team to set up those scoring opportunities.

First off, neuroscience shows us our brains can change based on what we focus on—this is called neuroplasticity. Every time you practice the steps of the Mind Matrix, you're training your brain to form new connections. It's like carving new pathways in a forest, making it easier to walk the path of positive thinking every time.

Romans 12:2 tells us not to conform to the patterns of this world but be transformed by renewing our minds. This is exactly what you're doing with the Mind Matrix! By using Truth Prime along with the other steps, you're filling your mind with God's truths and what He says about you, helping you to see and live out the great plans He has for you.

Here's how the Truth Prime and the other Mind Matrix components work together:

Recognize: You start by spotting the negative thoughts and beliefs that hold you back. It's like identifying the enemy plays in a game. This step is crucial because you can't change what you don't see.

Record: Then you get these thoughts down, either in a journal or as notes. This move makes you aware of the patterns you're dealing with, kind of like watching replays in sports to see what needs improvement.

Refute: This is where you challenge those negative thoughts, like a team coming up with a strategy to counter the opponent's moves. You use logical and mirror processes, finding evidence and your faith to prove these negative beliefs wrong.

Rewire (TRUTH Brain Prime): Here's the star play—replacing those old beliefs with new, positive truths about yourself. You make recordings in your own voice of these truths and listen to them daily. It's your brain's daily training session, reinforcing the positive beliefs so strongly that they become your new automatic thoughts, creating a new neural network toward your success.

Each step of the Mind Matrix prepares the ground for the Truth Brain Prime to be super effective. Just like practicing drills makes a sports team better, every part of the Mind Matrix makes your brain more receptive to the positive truths you're focusing on.

Neuroscience tells us that the more we repeat a thought or action, the stronger those brain pathways become. And scripture encourages us to fill our minds with whatever is true, noble, right, pure, lovely, and admirable (Philippians 4:8). By doing the Truth Prime along with the other steps, you're basically giving your brain a daily workout with God's truths, strengthening those pathways of positive, Godly thinking.

So, by integrating the Truth Prime with the rest of the Mind Matrix and aligning it with neuroscience and scripture, you're setting yourself up for some serious personal transformation. You're not just changing how you think; you're changing how you live, moving closer to the person God created you to be.

God tells us to renew our minds and take our thoughts captive.

As I wrap up this chapter, I want you to think about this: God tells us to renew our minds and take our thoughts captive. It's not about learning these things and then switching to autopilot. It's about actively managing our thoughts, the ones that could stop us dead in our tracks. Recognizing you're the creator—the master—of your thoughts is empowering. You're not just passively accepting random thoughts anymore. Now you're like the bouncer at the door of your mind, deciding who gets in and who gets bounced!

Embrace your role as a creator. You're taking charge of your thoughts, shaping your future, and living the life God intended for you. That's the power of the Mind Matrix—simple, yet incredibly transformative.

Step into your power as the architect of your thoughts and, by extension, your life. By mastering the Mind Matrix and embracing your role as a creator, you're not just dreaming about a better future; you're actively building it, living the abundant life that was always meant for you. This is the essence of the Mind Matrix: a journey of simplicity leading to profound transformation. You have released the brakes on your dreams!

10

Vision Brain Prime

Now, let's talk about Vision. It's time to dream big! I mean, sky's-the-limit big. Those dreams you're almost embarrassed to share because they're so huge? Write them down. We're talking about your Epic Audacious Goals here.

You might be thinking, "But Shannon, won't this put my brain into panic mode?" Normally, yes. But we're flipping the script! We're using the brain's systems to our advantage. First, jot down those big dreams in all areas of your life—business, relationships, health, spirituality, you name it.

These aren't just idle daydreams. We're setting the stage for your brain to start working toward these goals. Traditional goal setting, like setting SMART goals, stops short, triggering your fight-or-flight system that has your brain working against you. Not us. We're going full throttle, using these dreams to prime your brain for success.

Now that you've penned down your heart's desires in all life areas, we're about to switch gears. We're going to transform these dreams from distant wants into present, tangible realities. It's all about changing the language from "I want" and "It would be nice" to a vibrant, living present. Imagine it's already happening right now!

Take each dream, each goal, and repaint it with the colors of the present tense. Picture them as done deals. For instance, if you're dreaming of a seven-figure business, don't just say, "I want a business that makes millions." No, bring it to life! Say, "I run a seven-figure business that gives me the freedom to live life on my terms. I've just returned from my second sun-soaked vacation this year, one in Bora Bora and another in Costa Rica, and my business? It ran smoothly without me!" That's the power of training your brain to see it so that it helps you create it. This is WAY more than just visualization.

Take each dream, each goal, and repaint it with the colors of the present tense.

But don't stop there. Dive into the details. What does success taste like, feel like, smell like? Who's celebrating with you? What's the texture of the sand under your feet in Costa Rica? What perfume are you wearing as you toast to your achievements? Envision the weather, the laughter, the joy.

And think about the ripple effect. How has your success uplifted your clients, your family, your friends, and your significant other? It's not just about you; it's about the impact you're creating.

This is the essence of the Vision Brain Prime. It's about crafting a vision so vivid, so sensory-rich that your brain can't tell the difference between imagination and reality. It's about painting your future in such vibrant strokes that it becomes indistinguishable from the present. This isn't just dreaming big—it's living your dream in the here and now.

Alright, now I hear you asking, "Is this just another spin on affirmations?" Absolutely not. Affirmations are often these broad, one-size-fits-all statements that might not resonate with everyone's unique journey. What we're doing here is crafting specific, personal Vision Brain Prime—your own custom-made declarations based on your individual desires, dreams, and divine calling. This isn't about repeating generic mantras; it's about speaking your truth into existence. "Speak what is not yet as if it is already" (Romans 14:17). This is how God wired our brains to allow our calling to become reality.

The idea behind the Vision Brain Prime technique isn't just a cool trick. It's actually backed by some serious brain science that shows why picturing our goals like they've already happened can really help us achieve them.

THE SCIENCE OF THE BRAIN PRIME

Neuroplasticity: At the heart of the Brain Prime's effectiveness is the concept of neuroplasticity, the brain's ability to form and reorganize synaptic connections, especially in response to learning or experience. When you visualize achieving your goals, your brain forms connections as if those experiences were real. This means that regularly imagining your success can rewire your brain to recognize and pursue paths that lead to those achievements.

The Reticular Activating System (RAS): The RAS is a network of neurons located in the brainstem that plays a key role in controlling arousal and focusing attention. When you consistently see your goals as if they have already been achieved, you effectively program the RAS to filter information and opportunities that align with these goals. This enhances your ability to notice and seize opportunities that you might have otherwise overlooked.

Mirror Neurons: Research on mirror neurons—cells in the brain that fire not only when performing an action but also when observing an action performed by someone else—supports the power of the Vision Brain Prime. By vividly imagining your success, the mirror neurons activate in similar ways as they would if you were actually experiencing that success. This can improve skills and boost confidence, making it easier to take the steps needed to achieve your goals.

Stress Reduction and Performance Enhancement: Studies have shown that using a tool like the Brain Prime can reduce stress and anxiety, particularly related to performance in sports, public speaking, and exams. By imagining successful outcomes, individuals can enter a more relaxed and confident state, which is conducive to better performance. These practices are widely used in sports psychology to enhance athletic performance, demonstrating that mental rehearsals can be nearly as effective as physical practice.

Goal Achievement: Research in the field of positive psychology has highlighted the effectiveness of positive visualization in achieving goals. A study published in the *Journal of Positive Psychology* found that participants who engaged in positive-future-visualization exercises showed increased levels of motivation and took more initiative toward achieving their goals compared to those who did not.

LINDA'S STORY

Let's talk about Linda, a woman in her fifties with a dream tucked away in her heart—to become an author. Despite her burning passion for storytelling, doubts and the ticking clock made her question if it was too late to embark on such an ambitious journey. That was until she joined the 67-Day Year coaching program and discovered the power of the Vision Brain Prime technique, a method that promised to reshape her path to success.

Linda embarked on a unique journey with Brain Prime, where she began to actively listen to her Brain Prime morning and night. She would use her mind to see herself as the successful author she longed to be. She vividly imagined holding her published book in her hands, reading through pages of glowing reviews, and even standing proudly at her own book signing events.

With each session of Brain Prime, morning and night, Linda closed her eyes and painted these scenarios in her mind with such detail and emotion, it was as if they were already part of her reality. This practice ignited a significant shift within her. The self-doubt that once anchored her dreams to the shore of hesitation began to dissolve, making way for a steadfast belief in her potential and capabilities.

Fueled by the powerful imagery created through the Vision Brain Prime, Linda found herself more motivated than ever. She dedicated time every day to write, weaving her thoughts and stories into the tapestry of her budding book. She even reached out to join a writers' group, a step she had previously shied away from, seeking the support and feedback that would hone her craft further. Linda's dream was no longer a distant echo; it had begun to crystallize into a tangible goal.

A year of dedication, bolstered by the consistent practice of Vision Brain Priming, led to a moment Linda had replayed a thousand times in her mind—holding the first copy of her published book. The feeling of déjà vu enveloped her as she realized the scenes she had so vividly imagined had materialized into her reality. Linda's journey from dreaming to achieving stands as a powerful testament to the Vision Brain Prime technique. It showcased that when you combine the proactive action of Brain Prime with actual steps toward your goal, even the most ambitious dreams can be realized.

When you combine the proactive action of Brain Prime with actual steps toward your goal, even the most ambitious dreams can be realized.

This story illuminates a fundamental truth about the science behind how our brains work and the transformative potential of our imagination. By embedding our deepest aspirations into our consciousness as vivid, tangible realities through Brain Prime, we set the stage for our physical actions to align with these envisioned futures. It demonstrates that with the right mental preparation, our goals don't just remain figments of our imagination but evolve into achievable milestones, guiding us steadily toward the success we've always envisioned.

Let's break it down step by step:

CREATE YOUR VISION BRAIN PRIME

Step One

Jot down everything you're yearning for across various life domains. This includes your financial goals, relationship aspirations, spiritual connections, physical health, mental wellbeing, and even the nitty-gritty details of your daily environment. Think about your dream house, your ideal job, your cherished relationships—write it all out. What do your heart and soul truly desire? WHAT DO YOU WANT?!

Step Two

Now flip this wish list into the language of completion. Transform these dreams into statements that reflect they're already achieved. For example, instead of saying, "I want to live in Dana Point overlooking the ocean," say, "I am sitting in my beautiful Dana Point home, feeling the ocean breeze, overwhelmed with gratitude for the incredible journey God has led me on." This step is crucial—it's about training your brain to see your future as your current reality.

Guided Brain Prime Exercise

Let's dive into making your dreams feel real right now with a guided Brain Prime. This will help you see, feel, and believe in your goals as if they're already part of your life. Follow these steps to make your Vision Brain Prime super vivid and powerful:

Find a Quiet Space: Choose a quiet, comfortable spot where you won't be interrupted. This could be your room, a cozy corner, or even a peaceful spot outdoors.

Relax: Close your eyes and take a few deep breaths. Inhale slowly, hold it for a moment, and then exhale. Repeat this a few times until you feel your body relax.

Picture Your Achievements: Start with one goal from your Brain Prime list. Really imagine it's already happened. If your goal is to live in a beautiful home by the ocean, see yourself there. Imagine you're sitting in your living room, with big windows open to the sea.

Engage Your Senses:
- *See:* What does your Dana Point home look like? Notice the colors, the light filtering in, the furniture, and any art on the walls.
- *Hear:* Can you hear the ocean waves? Maybe there's music playing softly in the background, or the distant sound of seagulls.
- *Smell:* Breathe in the salty sea breeze, or maybe the aroma of your favorite meal cooking in the kitchen.

- *Touch:* Feel the softness of the sofa you're sitting on, the cool breeze against your skin, or the warmth of the sun coming through the window.
- *Taste:* Maybe you're sipping your favorite drink. What does it taste like?

Add Emotion: This is crucial. How do you feel sitting in your dream home? Filled with gratitude? Overflowing with joy? Relaxed and at peace? Really let those feelings wash over you.

Expand Your Vision: Think about how achieving this goal affects other areas of your life. Who's there with you? What new opportunities have opened up because of this achievement? How has it impacted your relationships, your health, or your career?

Deepening the Experience

Repetition Is Key: Practice this Brain Prime imagery regularly. The more you do it, the more real it will feel, and the more your brain will start to work toward making it a reality.

Write It Down: After your visualization, jot down anything new that came up or any details that felt particularly important. This can help make your vision even clearer over time. Add it to your Vision Brain Prime.

Ditch the Doubts: If doubts or negative thoughts pop up during your Brain Prime, acknowledge them and then let them go. Refocus on the positive feelings and the details of your achieved goal.

Vision Brain Priming isn't just daydreaming; it's a powerful tool for making your dreams come true. By vividly imagining your goals as already achieved, you're training your brain to believe in them and opening yourself up to the actions and opportunities that will make them a reality. Keep practicing, and don't be afraid to dream big. Your future is waiting for you to create it, one vivid Vision Brain Prime at a time.

Step Three

Grab your phone and hit record. Speak these visions out loud, pouring your passion, emotions, and belief into every word. Imagine you're narrating the story of your life, but it's the life you're going to live. Make sure your language reflects completion—there's no more "going to" or "will"; it's all happening right now. This isn't just reading off a script; it's declaring your destiny.

Now here's where the magic really starts to happen, echoing what God teaches us: persist in asking, seeking, and thinking. It's like God left us a blueprint in the Bible, and we're just now piecing it together. Step four is all about immersing yourself in your vision, listening to your recorded dreams first thing in the morning and last thing at night. Why? Because your brain is like a supercomputer at these times, sorting and filing away thoughts. By feeding it your vision at these critical moments, you're programming it to turn your dreams into your reality.

In the evening, as you're drifting off to sleep, your brain processes and prioritizes your thoughts from the day. It's the perfect time to reinforce your vision, seeding your subconscious with the blueprint of your future. And then, first thing in the morning, before the day's hustle begins, give your brain a refresher of what it's working toward. This primes your mind to look for opportunities and pathways to make your vision a tangible reality throughout the day.

For those who love a good workout—and I strongly suggest you join the club if you haven't already—listen to your Vision Brain Prime during your exercise routine. There's a reason why we often have those "aha" moments during physical activity or in the shower; it's when our conscious and subconscious minds are most relaxed and aligned. Use this time to strengthen the connection between your aspirations and your brain's processing power.

It's fascinating, isn't it? We often get caught up in constantly doing, chasing after strategies and tactics. Yet, both science and faith teach us that it's in the thinking, in the being, that the doing finds its roots. Our education system might have taught us *to do* in order *to be*, but in God's wisdom, it's the reverse. By faith, we are, and from our being springs forth our doing. The Brain Prime is our tool to align our thinking with our desired path, making it familiar and safe for our brains.

> *It's in the thinking, in the being, that the doing finds its roots.*

As you keep up with this practice, you reach a point—the 67th repetition, give or take—where your brain really starts to take notice. This is where the real transformation begins. The pathways in your brain start to realign, automating your new beliefs and visions into the subconscious. This is the pivotal moment when your Vision Brain Prime becomes an ingrained part of your decision-making process, guiding your actions and shaping your results.

INTEGRATING TRUTH PRIME

In the Mind Matrix chapter, we dove deep into recognizing, recording, and refuting those limiting beliefs. You became a lawyer of your own mind, dissecting and discarding the lies that held you back. From this process emerged your Truth Brain Prime, a powerful testament to both the logical and emotional truths that will replace the old, automated lies in your subconscious. Now it's time to bring this truth to life through the Truth Prime, an integral part of the Brain Prime system.

Imagine the Brain Prime system as a one-two punch. The first punch is the Vision Prime, where you automated your grand vision, infusing it with life and energy. The second punch, equally crucial, is the Truth Prime, where you solidify and internalize the truths you've unearthed. This is where you take your refute step from the Mind Matrix, read it aloud, and embrace its power. Remember the mirror exercise? This is where you flip the script from third person to first person, owning these truths as your own.

The process is beautifully straightforward. Record your Truth Prime, blending both the logical and emotional aspects. Listening to it becomes a daily ritual, just like the Vision Prime. I've noticed a common pitfall here—people love to focus on the Vision Prime because it's all about the bright, shiny future. But the past, with all its outdated scripts, dictates 90 percent or more of our decisions, actions, and results. Neglecting the Truth Prime is like trying to drive with one foot on the gas and the other on the brake—you won't get far.

POWER OF REPETITION

Now you're armed with the full power of the Brain Prime system. You know how to craft a belief, how to create a Vision Prime that's already fulfilled in your mind's eye, and how to dismantle and rewrite the old stories with your Truth Prime. You're not just dreaming of a future; you're actively sculpting it, choosing your truths by design, not by default.

Now, it all comes down to repetitions. The more you repeat your truth and vision primes, the stronger and more automatic they become, influencing 90 percent of your daily decisions and actions. That vigilant guard at the door of your subconscious, once wary of your dreams, now welcomes them as familiar and safe, paving the way for their realization.

The more you repeat your truth and vision primes, the stronger and more automatic they become.

Take Shelley, for instance. Initially, she was incredibly shy, yet she harbored a powerful message within. Through diligent Brain Priming, she began to see remarkable changes. She transformed from saying, "I'm not a speaker," to confidently affirming, "I am ready to speak on stages globally." In just two weeks, this shift led her to five speaking engagements and an incredible income boost. It's astounding how our own thoughts can be the biggest barricades to our success. Shelley's story exemplifies how quickly you can dismantle these barriers with the right mindset tools.

FAITH AND TRANSFORMATION

This rapid transformation aligns with God's vision for us. He has plans for our prosperity, for a hopeful and abundant future, both in the present and beyond. We are not meant to be hindered by our own doubts or the deceptions of the world. At the heart of it all, life boils down to two fundamental choices: faith and belief or fear and doubt. And it all starts with your thoughts. You are the master of your thoughts, and those thoughts craft your future.

Life boils down to two fundamental choices: faith and belief or fear and doubt.

Now that you're equipped with the entire SINC Neuro Coaching Model, you understand how beliefs are formed and transformed. You've seen what's been holding you back and learned how to dismantle those limitations. Most importantly, you know how to activate your brain's success switch.

The next section of our journey is about application—translating this newfound knowledge into your day-to-day life. With your vision taking shape and the Mind Matrix clearing your path, it's time to focus on achieving your goals. And yes, there is indeed a right and wrong way to do this. In the next chapter, we'll dive into strategies for efficient and effective goal attainment, avoiding the slow and painful routes. Get ready to embrace a life where your dreams aren't just possibilities, but imminent realities!

BRINGING IT ALL TOGETHER

Combining the 7 Whys with the Mind Matrix and Brain Prime techniques creates a super powerful toolkit for achieving your goals and dreams! Let's break down how these three strategies work together to help you achieve your dreams.

Step 1: Identify What You Want with the 7 Whys

First up, we have the 7 Whys, which is like a deep-dive exploration into why your goals matter to you. By asking "Why?" seven times, you're not just scratching the surface; you're digging deep to find out what truly drives you. This is like setting up the destination in your GPS before you start driving.

Step 2: Use the Mind Matrix to Break Free from Limitations

Next, the Mind Matrix comes into play. This method helps you spot any negative beliefs or obstacles that might be holding you back from achieving what you discovered in your 7 Whys. Think of this as identifying roadblocks and detours on your journey so you can find the best route to your destination.

Step 3: Create Your Brain Prime

Once you've got your destination locked in and you know what obstacles to avoid, it's time to use the Vision Brain Prime system. This is where you take the goals and desires you identified with the 7 Whys and start turning them into vivid, positive statements as if they've already happened. It's like creating a highlight reel of your future success to watch in your mind's eye.

How They Work Together

The 7 Whys help you figure out what you really want and why. This makes sure that your goals are deeply meaningful to you, which is crucial because the more personally significant a goal is, the more motivated you'll be to achieve it.

The Mind Matrix is like a cleanup crew for your mind. It helps you get rid of the doubts and fears uncovered during the 7 Whys process. By doing this, you clear a path for your true desires to shine through without anything holding them back.

Brain Priming is where you take the clear, obstacle-free path you've made and start paving it with gold. By repeatedly visualizing your success (based on the goals you set with the 7 Whys), you're telling your brain, "This is where we're going, and it's going to be amazing."

To make this whole process work really well, remember to:

Be Specific: The more details you can imagine, the better. If your goal is to become a successful author, imagine holding your book, reading fan letters, or seeing your name on the bestseller list.

Feel the Emotion: Don't just see it; feel it. Imagine the joy, pride, or sense of achievement you'll feel when you reach your goal. Emotions supercharge the Brain Prime process.

Repeat, Repeat, Repeat: Repetition is key. The more you go through this process, the stronger the pathways in your brain become, making it easier for you to move toward your goals.

Sometimes it can be tough to keep up with the practice, especially if you don't see immediate results. If you find yourself struggling:

Schedule It: Make it a nonnegotiable part of your day, like brushing your teeth.

Trust It: This is the brain science of success and you are flipping your brain's success switch on!

Stay Patient: Big changes don't happen overnight. Keep at it, and trust the process.

By integrating the 7 Whys with the Mind Matrix and Brain Prime, you're giving yourself a comprehensive roadmap to achieving your biggest goals and dreams. You understand your deepest motivations, clear away anything holding you back, and regularly reinforce a positive vision of your future. This combination is like rocket fuel for your goals, propelling you toward the life you've always wanted.

This is the essence of creating a life by design, not by default. If you don't consciously choose your path, you'll end up living someone else's. So let's move forward with intention, setting Epic Audacious Goals that reflect our true desires and purpose.

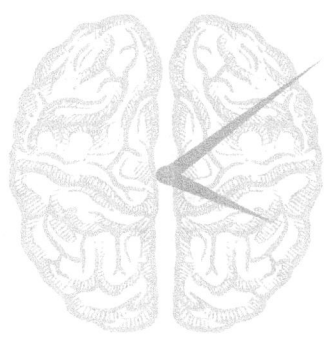

PART THREE

The 67-Day Year Method

*Creating a Year's Worth
of Goals in 67 Days*

11

Developing Your Vision

Creating Your Epic Audacious Goals (EAG)

Oh, if only the world could be created in a day, if only the universe could reveal its glory faster than a lifetime. By now, you're familiar with the power of the number 67. You know that 67 days is what it takes to create an incredible prime in your mind. But did you know that in Hebrew, the number 67 signifies completion or transformation? It's mind-blowing that the same number of days required to create a new pathway in your brain is also the number for transformation. God truly has a sense of humor and a way of providing confirmation, doesn't He?

When we talk about goals, we often think about things like getting a new job, losing weight, or saving money for a vacation. These are great targets, but there's something even bigger and more exciting that can really change the game—Epic Audacious Goals (EAG). An EAG isn't just any goal; it's your BIG VISION, the ultimate destination of success that feels almost too big to dream about. It's the kind of goal that gives you goosebumps just thinking about it because it represents the pinnacle of what you believe is possible for your life.

EAGs are important because they push you beyond your comfort zone. They make you stretch further than you thought you could, sparking growth and transformation along the way. While regular goals are like steps on a ladder, helping you climb higher step by step, an EAG is like seeing the whole skyscraper you're aiming to reach. It's your true north, guiding all your efforts and helping you make decisions that align with your ultimate vision of success. To be honest, this is what you have really been dreaming about, maybe the desire that God has put in your heart.

THE DIFFERENCE BETWEEN EAGS AND REGULAR GOALS

The main difference between an EAG and regular goals is the scale and the impact. Regular goals might be achieved in the short to medium term and are often more practical and immediate. An EAG, on the other hand, is more about the long-term vision for your life or career. It's audacious and epic because it represents a culmination of your deepest desires and aspirations, often requiring significant time, effort, and perseverance to achieve.

Your EAG represents a culmination of your deepest desires and aspirations.

Take Sarah, for example. She always dreamed of opening a network of schools in underserved communities around the world. Her Epic Audacious Goal wasn't just to impact her local community but to transform education on a global scale. While her friends and family initially doubted such a grand vision, Sarah broke down her EAG into smaller, actionable steps, starting with volunteering, then teaching, and eventually studying educational development.

Years of dedication, learning, and networking later, Sarah launched her first school in a remote community, using innovative teaching methods tailored to the community's needs. That first school became the model for others, leading to a network of schools across several countries, changing thousands of lives. Sarah's story shows that even the most ambitious Epic Audacious Goals are achievable when pursued with passion, perseverance, and a strategic approach—and the 67-Day Year tools!

THE NEUROSCIENCE BEHIND ACHIEVING GOALS

Neuroscience tells us that when we set goals, our brain works in fascinating ways to help us achieve them. The brain loves clarity, and when we break down our EAG into smaller, manageable steps, it helps create a clear path for our brain to follow. This is because of the Reticular Activating System (RAS), which helps filter relevant information and opportunities that align with our goals.

Achieving smaller goals on the way to an EAG releases dopamine, a neurotransmitter associated with pleasure and motivation. This keeps us motivated and reinforces our commitment to the larger vision. Setting and working toward an EAG not only gives us a profound sense of purpose but also aligns with the brain's natural process of goal achievement through incremental progress.

An Epic Audacious Goal isn't just a dream; it's a vision of the highest level of success that you can imagine for yourself. It's powerful because it encompasses your deepest aspirations and defines what true success means to you. By understanding and applying the principles of neuroscience to break your EAG into micro-steps, you can systematically work your way toward this grand vision, turning what once seemed impossible into reality. Remember, every big achievement starts with the courage to dream big. So dare to set your own EAG and embark on the journey to make it come to life.

Next, we're going to talk about how to set goals and accomplish the tasks needed to achieve them daily, all while aligning with how the brain allows for results. And I'm going to encapsulate it in one word: micro.

MACRO TO MICRO

We used macro when creating our Brain Prime, defining everything we wanted and removing all limitations. Now we're going to switch to the language of the brain, which is micro. This shift enables you to tap into the brain's micro system, ensuring you never put your brain in a state of overwhelm or fight-or-flight again. Goodbye, overwhelm; it's not been nice knowing you.

To go micro, you get the neurochemicals working for you. Remember, if these neurochemicals aren't on our side, they'll sound the alarm bell that this is not safe and familiar. So let's dive into how we can set Epic Audacious Goals and break them down into manageable, micro steps.

When my husband and I were hiking Mount Whitney, we hired a guide to help us navigate the mountain. Another group of younger guys started at the same time, charging straight up the face of the mountain. As we took a winding path with our guide, what seemed like an overwhelming mountain at first became a series of manageable boulders. This experience mirrored how the brain can get overwhelmed by the big picture but can handle smaller, micro tasks more easily.

> *The brain can get overwhelmed by the big picture but can handle smaller, micro tasks more easily.*

As we continued our ascent, the boulders became smaller rocks, and eventually, pebbles. When we reached the top, the once-daunting mountain now appeared as a series of small steps stacked upon each other. This is a perfect analogy for how the brain allows for micro achievements while perceiving macro goals as threats. That's why we focus on micro rather than macro.

DEFINING YOUR MOUNTAIN: YOUR EAG FOR THE YEAR

But first, we need to define your mountain, your Epic Audacious Goal for the year. What's the one big thing that, if accomplished this year, would be a game changer for you? This goal should be significant enough to excite you and perhaps even scare you a bit. Take a moment to reflect on what this could be for you.

A lifetime EAG represents your ultimate aspiration, a beacon that guides your life's work and passion, such as revolutionizing education in underprivileged areas worldwide. In contrast, an annual EAG focuses on a significant milestone achievable within a year, like launching a pioneering online course that lays the groundwork for your lifetime vision of educational transformation.

Setting Your EAG for the Year

To set your sights on your own EAG for the year, it's essential to pinpoint that monumental ambition that can pivot the direction of your life. Here's a step-by-step guide to help you identify your EAG, peppered with probing questions and criteria to ensure your goal is both ambitious and achievable.

Step 1: Dream Big

Start by allowing yourself to dream without limits. Imagine that you have all the resources, time, and energy needed. What would you aim for?

Question to Ask: If I knew I couldn't fail, what would I pursue this year?

Step 2: Reflect on Your Values

Your EAG should resonate deeply with your personal values and long-term vision. Reflect on what matters most to you in life.

Criteria to Consider: Does this goal align with my core values and the legacy I want to leave? Does it align with my 7 Whys?

Step 3: Assess the Impact

Consider how achieving this goal will transform your life. Think about the broader impact on your relationships, career, and personal growth.

Question to Ask: How will achieving this goal change my life and the lives of those around me?

Step 4: Define Your Fear Factor

An EAG should stretch your limits and push you out of your comfort zone. Identify a goal that's exciting but also a bit intimidating.

Criteria to Consider: Does thinking about this goal give me a mix of excitement and nervousness?

Step 5: Set a Timeline

While your EAG is for the year, breaking it down into smaller milestones can make it more tangible and achievable.

Question to Ask: What are the key milestones I need to achieve along the way to reach my EAG?

Let's say you are an online coach. Here's what your Lifetime and Annual EAGs might look like:

Lifetime Entrepreneurial EAG for an Online Coach: Establishing a leading online coaching platform that transforms the lives of millions globally by providing accessible, high-quality personal and professional development resources.

Annual Entrepreneurial EAG for an Online Coach: Launching a signature coaching program that reaches over 1,000 participants in its first year, providing them with the tools to achieve breakthroughs in their personal and professional lives, thereby laying the foundation for the platform's global reach.

Identifying your EAG is the first monumental step in the 67-Day Year method that promises transformation and growth. Your EAG will not only challenge you but also inspire you to push beyond your perceived limits. As you ponder your EAG, remember that the journey toward this goal is equally important. It will be filled with learning, growth, and moments of self-discovery.

In the next chapter, we'll dive into creating a roadmap for achieving your EAG. We'll discuss strategies for breaking down your EAG into manageable actions, overcoming obstacles, and staying motivated on your journey to transformation. Get ready to turn your Epic Audacious Goal from a dream into your reality.

12

Breaking Down the Vision

From Mountains to Boulders

Just like on our Mount Whitney hike, when we got partway up the mountain, we noticed that boulders were really what made up the mountain. So, what are your boulders—the ten or so essential things you must do to make your mountain a reality?

For example, maybe your BIG EAG (mountain) is like my client Sam's, who wanted to create a business that brought in enough income for her to quit her 9–5 job, stop trading time for money, and spend more time with her two- and four-year-old kids. She knew she wanted it badly and why. We worked with her in the 67-Day Year coaching program to help her create MICRO steps—BOULDERS.

In our journey to achieve big dreams, like climbing a mountain, we often find that it's not just a smooth path upward but made up of boulders and rocks that we need to navigate. This is a great way to think about reaching our EAGs, or as we call it, our mountain. To make it to the top, it's not just about knowing where you want to go but understanding the specific steps, or "boulders," and even smaller actions, or "micro steps," that will get you there.

> **Boulders—The Big Steps:** Think of boulders as the big, essential tasks you need to accomplish to reach your goal. These are significant milestones that require effort and determination to overcome but are crucial for making progress. For example, if your mountain is to start a business, a boulder might be creating your business plan, securing financing, or developing your first product.

> **Rocks—The Medium Steps:** While boulders are big tasks, "rocks" are the medium-sized steps that support those larger tasks. They are important but not as monumental as boulders. Continuing with the business example, a rock could be conducting market research to inform your business plan or setting up business bank accounts for your financing.

> **Pebbles—The Micro Steps:** Micro steps are the smallest, most actionable tasks that lead to completing a rock or boulder. These are specific, day-to-day actions that are easy to achieve and help build momentum. For Sam, who wants to start a business to have more time with her kids, a micro step could be dedicating one hour each day to researching her target market or setting up a daily reminder to sketch out ideas for her product.

Imagine Sam's EAG is to start her online coaching business. Here's how her journey might break down:

- **Boulder:** Develop her first coaching offer.
- **Rock** (part of the "Develop her first coaching offer" boulder): Create a outline of her coaching offer—what will be included.
- **Pebbles or Micro Steps** (part of the "Create a coaching offer outline of her" rock): Spend 30 minutes each morning brainstorming steps in her coaching method.

By breaking down her EAG into boulders, rocks, and pebbles or micro steps, Sam can take consistent, manageable actions toward her goal. This approach not only makes the journey less overwhelming but also allows for regular progress checks and adjustments as needed.

IDENTIFYING YOUR BOULDERS

Understanding and implementing the distinction between boulders, rocks, and pebbles is key to achieving any large goal. It transforms the seemingly insurmountable task of moving a Mountain into a series of achievable actions, bringing you closer to your dream with each step you take.

Sam determined that she needed to first grow an audience and then sell to them, so she focused on growing her audience as the boulder that would allow her to create a 150K+ year coaching business. As she did, she no longer fell into overwhelm, which had stopped her in her tracks for the last five years. She did not look at anything else but her BOULDER (and rocks and pebbles). Her boulder: grow an audience of two hundred people. Her outcome was mind-blowing—more on that story later.

So, what are your boulders? If you want to create a business that replaces your income, maybe one of the boulders to becoming a coach is to get certified, and maybe another boulder is to offer your coaching services. Maybe another boulder is to speak on other people's podcasts. Take some time with this one. What are ten, no more than twelve but usually around ten, big boulders that would make up that mountain and, like dominoes, start to make that mountain possible?

Tips for Identifying Your Key Boulders

Identifying your key boulders is a crucial step in turning your EAG into a reality. These boulders are the foundational tasks that will propel you toward your dream, so choosing them wisely and strategically is important. Here are some tips and questions to help you pinpoint what these boulders might be for you:

Identifying your key boulders is a crucial step in turning your EAG into a reality.

> **Reflect on the End Goal:** What does success look like for my EAG? Picture your goal in detail—what have you achieved, and how do you know you've succeeded?

> **Break Down the Goal:** Start with your EAG goal and work backwards. List all the major steps you believe are necessary to get there. Don't worry about ordering them yet; just get them on paper.

Evaluate the Impact: Which of these tasks will have the most significant impact on reaching my goal? Consider which boulders, once moved, will make other steps easier or even unnecessary.

Prioritize Your List: Once you've listed potential boulders, prioritize them based on their impact and what feels right to start with. You're looking for a balance between what's most effective and what's achievable to keep momentum.

Reflect on Your Passion and Skills: Which of these boulders excites me the most? Which align with my current skills, and which might require new learning or help? Your motivation and existing skills can be deciding factors in what to tackle first.

Revisit and Revise: Your list of boulders is not set in stone. As you progress toward your goal, you'll learn more, and your strategy may need to adjust. Be flexible and willing to update your boulders as needed.

By taking the time to carefully consider and identify your key boulders, you set a strong foundation for your journey toward achieving your EAG. Remember, each boulder moved gets you one step closer to the peak of your mountain.

EMBRACING THE PROCESS

These are your boulders, and you can already feel there's so much more peace around them. When you look at the big mountain, like "I'm going to create a six-figure business," you start to put your brain into overwhelm. But when you see the boulders as "I just need to get certified," that certification will give you the knowledge and the steps to build your business. Then you're just focusing on the certification versus the entire business. And now your brain starts to relax a little bit, bringing dopamine back in and allowing you to feel good because you know, "It's only one step I need to take." It allows your brain to reduce the chemicals that stop you.

Neuroscience has shown that our brains are capable of neuroplasticity, which is the brain's ability to form and reorganize synaptic connections, especially in response to learning or experience. This means that when we engage in the process of planning and executing the steps toward our goals (our boulders), we're actually rewiring our brain to better align with these objectives, making it more adept at recognizing opportunities and solutions related to these goals.

Neuroplasticity is the brain's ability to form and reorganize synaptic connections.

When you focus on your boulders, you're effectively programming your RAS to highlight information and opportunities that will help you achieve your goals. This neural process supports the importance of clear, focused goals, as it guides your attention and resources toward achieving them. Science and Scripture agree on the power of this process!

Habakkuk 2:2 (NIV): "Then the Lord replied: 'Write down the revelation and make it plain on tablets so that a herald may run with it.'" This passage emphasizes the importance of clearly defining and documenting your visions and goals. By identifying your boulders and writing them down, you're making your goals "plain," which is crucial for both remembering them and taking actionable steps toward them.

Philippians 4:13 (NIV): "I can do all this through him who gives me strength." This verse supports the idea of pursuing ambitious goals. It reminds us that with faith and determination, we are capable of overcoming the challenges (or moving the boulders) that lie on the path to our EAGs. It underscores the importance of relying on spiritual strength to achieve what may seem impossible.

James 2:26 (NIV): "As the body without the spirit is dead, so faith without deeds is dead." This scripture highlights the necessity of action. Identifying your boulders is only the first step; actively working toward them is essential. Faith in your ability to achieve your EAGs, combined with the diligent effort to move each boulder, are what lead to success.

These insights from neuroscience and the wisdom found in scripture shows that by focusing on your goals and taking actionable steps toward them, supported by faith and the understanding of our brain's capabilities, you can navigate the path to success more effectively.

ONE BOULDER: 67 DAYS

Now that you've identified all the significant tasks needed to achieve your Epic Audacious Goal—the boulders that make up the mountain—it's time to choose just one. Which one is the domino boulder? The one that, once accomplished, will make all the other boulders easier to tackle or even obsolete? Remember, there's no wrong choice here. Just pick one that feels like the right starting point for you.

MY FIRST BOULDER IS:

With your one boulder selected, your brain is relaxed. But we need to go even more micro. We know how to prime our brain with Truth and Vision Brain Prime, but we also need to take specific actions to achieve our goals. And that's where we often get overwhelmed by long to-do lists. But don't worry, we're about to break it down even further.

ROCKS

Your boulder is now rock-solid (pun intended), but what will make that boulder happen? These are your ROCKS—the major tasks that will accomplish the boulder. Come up with a list of ten to twenty major rocks, then put them in domino order. Your brain will start to see this as manageable, not a threat.

For example, Angelica shared her milestone achievement of nearing a $400,000 year in revenue, with 90 percent coming from low-ticket offers and her $47/month membership. She's determined to hit this goal before the year ends and is open to coaching to reach the finish line.

With your one boulder and its rocks outlined, confidence and encouragement are rising. Now grab some post-it notes (yes, physical post-its, not digital ones) and brainstorm all the actions, connections, and steps needed to accomplish that boulder. Each post-it should represent a task that takes 30 minutes or less. Break down any larger tasks into smaller parts.

Diving into the details of achieving your EAG means getting up close and personal with the tasks at hand—the rocks that pave the way to moving your big boulder. By using post-it notes for each action step, you make the whole process more manageable and less daunting. Let's explore what those post-it notes could look like, using the example of someone, let's call them Alex, whose boulder is to launch an online coaching business.

Here's what Alex's post-it notes might look like:

- *Research Coaching Certifications:* Spend 30 minutes googling different certification programs.
- *Outline Business Plan:* Break down the business plan into sections and spend 30 minutes outlining one section, like "Services Offered."
- *Brainstorm Business Names:* Set a timer for 30 minutes and jot down all the potential names for the coaching business.
- *Set Up a LinkedIn Profile:* Dedicate 30 minutes to updating or creating a LinkedIn profile focusing on coaching skills and goals.

- *Identify Potential Clients:* Spend 30 minutes listing people in your network who might benefit from your coaching services.
- *Sketch Logo Ideas:* Use 30 minutes to draw some basic logo concepts for your business on paper.
- *Research Web Hosting Services:* Allocate 30 minutes to look up the best web hosting platforms for your coaching website.
- *Create a Budget:* Break down your startup costs and spend 30 minutes starting a budget spreadsheet.
- *List Marketing Strategies:* Dedicate 30 minutes to listing out potential marketing strategies, like social media or email marketing.
- *Draft Introductory Email:* Spend 30 minutes writing an email template you can use to introduce your services to potential clients.

Each of these post-it notes represents a micro task that's part of a larger rock necessary to move Alex's boulder of launching an online coaching business. By breaking down each major task into smaller, more digestible pieces, Alex can tackle them one at a time without feeling overwhelmed. Here are some tips for creating your own:

- **Be Clear:** Each post-it should have a clear, actionable task that leaves no room for ambiguity about what needs to be done.
- **Be Realistic:** Ensure that the task can realistically be completed in 30 minutes or less. If it can't, break it down further.

- **Keep Going:** Write the post-it notes until you run out of ideas.
- **Break it Down:** If the item on the post-it is longer than 30 minutes, make several from the one post-it. For example: start a podcast (break that down into 30-minute steps).

This approach not only helps in organizing your steps toward achieving your boulder but also provides a visual sense of accomplishment as you remove or mark each post-it as done. It's a powerful way to keep motivation high and make consistent progress toward your big vision.

Once you have your pile of post-its, you have a visual representation of the steps to accomplish your boulder. In the next section, I'll show you how to arrange your post-its in a way that brings order to your brain and even more freedom to your day.

ARRANGING YOUR POST-ITS

Arranging your post-its—each representing a critical rock or task toward achieving your boulder—in a specific order is more than just an organizational strategy; it's a psychological tool that can significantly influence the success of your goal. This method brings clarity, focus, and a sense of direction to what might otherwise feel like an overwhelming journey. Here's why putting your rocks in order is crucial:

Clarity: When you lay out your tasks in a structured sequence, it's like plotting a route on a map. You can see where you're starting, the steps along the way, and where you'll end up. This clarity removes the guesswork from what to do next, making it easier to start and maintain momentum.

Focus: Having a specific order to follow helps narrow your focus to one task at a time, which is essential for deep work and productivity. Instead of scattering your energy across multiple tasks, you can channel it into completing the task at hand before moving on to the next.

Reduced Overwhelm: Looking at a mountain of tasks without any order can be daunting and stress-inducing. By arranging your tasks, you're essentially breaking down the mountain into manageable sections. This helps reduce feelings of overwhelm and makes the overall goal seem more achievable.

Prioritization: Ordering your tasks allows you to prioritize them based on importance, urgency, or logical progression. This ensures that critical tasks that have the most significant impact on your goal are completed first, thereby maximizing your efforts and resources.

Time Management: With your tasks laid out sequentially, you can better estimate the time required for each and plan your schedule accordingly. This aids in effective time management, allowing you to allocate your time to where it's needed most.

Momentum and Motivation: Each task you complete in the designated order is a small win that builds confidence and boosts motivation. Seeing the visual progress as you move through your post-its can be incredibly satisfying and encouraging, propelling you forward toward your larger goal.

Flexibility: While having an order is crucial, it also allows for flexibility. As you progress, you might find that some tasks need to be rearranged based on new information or changing circumstances. This adaptable structure ensures that your plan is always aligned with your goal's current reality.

Organizing your rocks in a specific order is a strategic move that can greatly influence your success in achieving your boulder. It transforms a chaotic pile of tasks into a streamlined, efficient pathway to your goal, empowering you with focus, clarity, and motivation. In the next section, we'll delve into practical ways to arrange your post-its, bringing even more order to your brain and freedom to your day, paving the way for the achievement of your EAG.

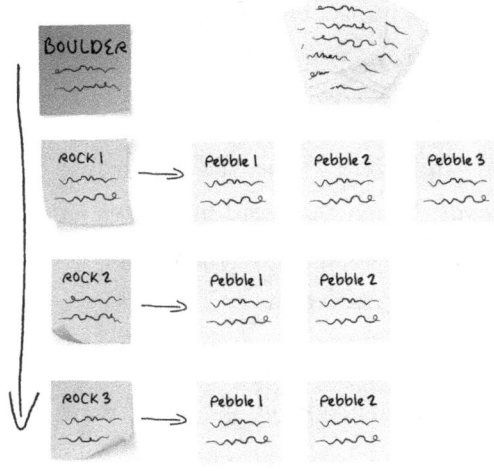

THE PATH

You've identified your mountain (your EAG), your boulders, and you've chosen a boulder to focus on. Now, with a pile of post-its in front of you, you're actively creating a life by design, not by default. Take a moment to recognize the power you've always had within you.

Here's something crucial to understand: you already knew what to do. When you created your Vision Brain Prime and your Truth Prime, you tapped into your intuition and that inner knowing. As you outlined your mountain and boulders, that same intuition guided you. This intuitive knowing, often overlooked in traditional education, is a God-given gift meant to guide you on your path.

Intuition is like having an inner GPS that guides you toward your biggest dreams, such as reaching your EAG. It's that feeling or gut instinct that tells you which path to take, even when it doesn't totally make sense logically. Trusting this intuition is really important. Sometimes, we stop listening to this inner voice because we think we should always make decisions based on facts and logic. But actually, your intuition is a powerful tool that helps you make the right choices.

To get in touch with your intuition, try to find quiet moments for yourself. This could be through prayer, meditation, being in nature, or just sitting quietly without any distractions. These quiet times let your intuition or inner voice speak up. When you're thinking about what steps to take toward your goal, ask yourself how you feel about

To get in touch with your intuition, try to find quiet moments for yourself.

each option rather than what you should do. Pay attention to how your body reacts and what emotions come up.

Writing down your thoughts and feelings can also help you understand your intuition better. Don't worry about making it perfect; just let your thoughts flow onto the paper. You might be surprised by what you discover.

You can also practice using your inner voice by making small decisions with it and seeing what happens. This helps you trust your intuition more, especially for the bigger decisions in life.

Make sure the choices you make based on your intuition are also in line with what's really important to you and what you really want out of life. When your intuition matches up with your true self and what you aim to achieve, it becomes an even stronger guide.

Sometimes, the hardest part is not doubting your intuition. If you start to question it, remind yourself of times when following your gut feeling led to the right outcome. Keep these memories as proof that your intuition is trustworthy.

Intuition isn't just about making decisions; it's a powerful force that, when combined with action and planning, can help you achieve great things. It's like mixing the knowledge of your brain with the wisdom of your heart. By listening to and trusting your inner voice, you're making choices that are best for you and moving closer to your big dream, your EAG, ensuring that you're creating a life by design, not by default.

As we progress, we'll discuss how to seek the right kind of learning when you're unsure of the next steps. But for now, appreciate how your intuition has already illuminated the steps you need to take. If you encounter a step that's unclear, remember that your intuition can also guide you to the right "who"—the person who can help you figure out the "how."

Intuition is a superpower bestowed by God, designed to lead you to your purpose. Remember, God has plans for you—plans for prosperity and hope. He gave you intuition to navigate the way from a mere pile of ideas to a clear path forward.

FROM A PILE TO A PATH

The brain thrives on clarity, order, and process. It's wired to follow a structured path. This is why traditional goal setting, which often relies on the whims of the day, can fall short. Now, with your pile of post-its, it's time to create a clear path forward.

> *The brain thrives on clarity, order, and process.*

As you sift through your post-its, you'll notice themes and categories emerging. Perhaps some tasks are related to gaining visibility, while others focus on networking or content creation. To organize these, find a blank wall and start grouping your post-its into related clusters. Each cluster will represent a category, such as "Podcast," "Visibility," or "Networking."

This is where the magic of the 67-Day Year Method comes into play. As you arrange your tasks, you'll begin to see the natural order in which they should be tackled. For instance, you can't record a podcast episode without first having the right equipment. So, start to sequence your tasks within each category, identifying what needs to be done first, second, and so on.

ORDERING THE STEPS

The brain craves clarity and order. It's designed to follow a process. Unlike traditional goal setting, where decisions are often governed by the what others want, we're now creating a clear path from the pile of post-its.

As you group your post-its into categories, you'll start to see patterns and processes emerge. This is where the magic happens. Begin to order the steps within each category, determining what needs to be accomplished first, second, third, and so on. Some tasks may not have a specific order, and that's okay. But for those that do, it's crucial to sequence them correctly.

This process of ordering your steps is like breaking down a giant mountain into manageable boulders, then further into specific steps to conquer each boulder, and finally into the order of steps to tackle those tasks. It's about taking what seemed overwhelming and breaking it down into clear, achievable steps.

Once you start sorting your post-it notes into groups, you'll notice patterns. This is where things start to get exciting. You'll see which step needs to come first, which comes next, and so on. Not every task needs to go in a certain order, but for the ones that do, putting them in the right sequence is super important.

Think of it like this: you're breaking down a huge mountain into big rocks (those are your main tasks). Then you're figuring out exactly what you need to do to move each of those rocks, making what felt impossible suddenly doable.

Now, life likes to throw surprises our way, and sometimes things don't go as planned. Maybe a task takes longer than you thought, or an unexpected challenge pops up. That's totally normal, and it's why being flexible is key. If you hit a roadblock or something's taking forever, it's okay to switch things up. Maybe there's a different task you can work on first, or maybe it's time to rethink your approach to a problem. The important thing is to keep moving forward, even if it's just tiny steps at a time.

Remember to start by making a big pile of post-its for all your tasks. Sort them into groups to see the big picture. Then, put the tasks in each group in the best order to tackle them. And when things don't go as planned, be ready to adjust.

Here's a little motivation to get you going: you have the power to climb your mountain, one step at a time. Each post-it note you tackle gets you closer to the top. So take a deep breath, trust in your plan, and start taking those steps. Your mountain is waiting, and you've got what it takes to reach the summit.

You have the power to climb your mountain, one step at a time.

13

The Daily Big Three

Going Micro

Now it's time to go micro with the daily big three. This is where the real magic happens. But first, a gut check: Have you been listening to your Brain Prime, both Vision and Truth, in the morning and evening? These primes are the foundation for everything we're doing. Without them, the steps we're taking won't matter.

The journey toward achieving your Epic Audacious Goal (EAG) narrows down to the daily actions you take, which we call the daily big three. This focused approach is where you'll see your dreams start turning into reality.

VISION BRAIN PRIME = YOUR EAG

Your Vision Brain Prime is a vivid, detailed imagination of your EAG as if it's already been achieved. It's picturing yourself living in that dream house, running your successful business, or celebrating a personal milestone. For example, if your EAG is to become a renowned public speaker, your Vision Brain Prime could be visualizing yourself on stage, speaking confidently to a packed auditorium, feeling the applause, and seeing the impact of your words on the audience. By listening to or mentally going through this Vision Prime every morning and evening, you align your subconscious mind with your goals, setting a positive tone for your day and reinforcing your objectives before you sleep.

TRUTH BRAIN PRIME

Your Truth Brain Prime is a set of truths that counter any lies or limiting beliefs you have about yourself and reinforce your ability to achieve your EAG. These affirmations speak to your capabilities, worth, and determination. For example, if doubt creeps in about your ability to succeed in business, your truth Brain Prime could be, "I am fully capable of creating and running a successful business. I bring unique value to my customers, and I overcome challenges with resilience and creativity." By repeatedly listening to or reciting these truths, you fortify your mindset against negativity and self-doubt, ensuring your actions are rooted in confidence and self-belief.

Using Your Brain Prime

To make the most of your Brain Prime, integrate them into your daily routine. Listen to your recorded primes and take time to vividly imagine and affirm them every morning when you wake up and every evening before you go to bed. This consistent practice embeds these visions and truths deep into your subconscious, influencing your thoughts and actions throughout the day and over time, aligning your daily reality with your ultimate goals.

Now, with a solid foundation set by your Vision and Truth Brain Prime, you're primed (pun intended) to focus on your daily big three—the specific, impactful actions you'll take each day to move closer to your EAG. Remember, the power of your journey lies in the daily, consistent steps informed and inspired by the deep connection to your goals established through your Brain Prime.

Your thoughts are the foundation on which everything is built. It's like the difference between building on solid rock and shifting sand.

Your thoughts are the foundation on which everything is built.

We have heard the parable of building a house on shifting sand rather on solid rock and only one stand the test of time. This analogy serves as a powerful metaphor for the importance of a strong foundation in achieving your goals. Just as a house needs a sturdy base to withstand storms and the test of time, your aspirations and dreams require a solid foundation of positive, empowering thoughts to thrive and succeed.

When you build on solid rock, it means grounding your goals in a mindset of resilience, positivity, and determination. Solid rock represents the robust and unwavering beliefs in your capabilities and the worthiness of your dreams. It's about having a clear vision, supported by Truth Brain Prime, that guides your actions and decisions. Like a house built on rock, your journey toward your goals remains stable and secure, even when faced with challenges and setbacks. This solid foundation ensures that you can weather the storms of doubt, fear, and external circumstances without crumbling.

On the other hand, building on shifting sand is akin to basing your efforts on doubts, fears, and negative self-talk. Shifting sand symbolizes a weak foundation of uncertain and negative thoughts that can easily be eroded by obstacles, criticism, or failures. Goals set upon this unstable ground are likely to collapse under pressure because they lack the resilience and strength provided by a positive mindset. Without a solid foundation, it's difficult to maintain direction and momentum, and the path to achieving your dreams becomes obscured and treacherous.

Just as a well-built house on solid rock remains standing through storms, a strong mental foundation allows you to persevere through challenges without giving up on your goals. You're strengthened by:

- **Clarity and Focus:** Building on solid rock provides a clear, stable base from which to direct your efforts. It ensures your actions are aligned with your vision and truth, keeping you focused on what matters most.
- **Growth:** A solid foundation supports growth. With a positive and resilient mindset, you're more open to learning from experiences, taking calculated risks, and expanding beyond your comfort zone.
- **Achievement:** Ultimately, a strong foundation increases the likelihood of achieving your goals. It transforms the journey into a more manageable and rewarding experience, paving the way for success.

The analogy of building on solid rock versus shifting sand underscores the critical role your thoughts and mindset play in the pursuit of your goals. By nurturing a foundation of positive, empowering beliefs and visions, you equip yourself with the strength and resilience needed to navigate the path to your dreams. Remember, the quality of your foundation determines not just the stability of your journey, but also the height of your achievements.

We need to ensure our foundation is strong by reinforcing it with our Truth and Vision Brain Primes.

THE POWER OF THREE: PRIORITIZING YOUR DAY

Now let's focus on the time of day when you're at your best. For most, it's the morning, but if you're a night owl, adjust accordingly. The key is to avoid letting other people's priorities hijack your most valuable time. Instead of starting your day by checking your phone and getting lost in emails or social media, dedicate the first part of your day to your God-given calling.

Here's the challenge: Choose three post-it tasks, each taking no more than 30 minutes, and commit to completing them before anything else. This is your daily big three. By focusing on these tasks, you're taking concrete steps toward your goals without overwhelming your brain. And remember, the order of these tasks is already laid out, thanks to the work you've done organizing your post-its.

Identifying Your Daily Big Three

Identifying your daily big three is like picking the juiciest fruits from a tree. You want to choose tasks that will give you the most satisfaction and move you closer to your goals.

Start by reviewing your list of post-it tasks and identifying those that are most urgent or important. These are the tasks that will have the biggest impact on your progress and should take top priority.

Next, consider the time and resources required for each task. Choose three tasks that you can realistically complete within 30 minutes each. This ensures that you're setting yourself up for success and avoiding overwhelm.

Finally, trust your intuition. If a task keeps nagging at you or feels especially meaningful, it's probably worth including in your daily big three. Your gut instinct is a powerful guide when it comes to prioritizing your time and energy.

By following these strategies, you'll be able to confidently choose your daily big three and make the most of your most valuable time each day.

Make the most of your most valuable time each day.

So, what are your daily big three? Write them down the night before, and tackle them first thing in the morning. This approach ensures that you're making progress on your goals every single day, setting the foundation for a life of intention and success.

Staying Focused During Your Daily Big Three

Staying focused during your daily big three is like keeping your eyes on the prize in a crowded room. Here are some tips to help you minimize distractions and stay on track:

Create a distraction-free environment: Find a quiet space where you can work without interruptions. Turn off notifications on your phone and computer, and let others know that you're unavailable during this time.

Use time-blocking techniques: Set a specific time period for each task and stick to it. Use a timer to help you stay on track and avoid spending too much time on any one task.

Break tasks into smaller steps: If a task feels overwhelming, break it down into smaller, more manageable steps. This can make it easier to stay focused and make progress.

Take breaks: Schedule short breaks between tasks to rest and recharge. Use this time to stretch, take a walk, or do something enjoyable to give your brain a break before moving on to the next task.

Reflect and adjust: At the end of each day, take a few minutes to reflect on your progress. Celebrate your accomplishments and identify any challenges or obstacles you encountered. Adjust your plans for the next day accordingly, making sure to prioritize tasks that will help you stay on track toward your goals.

By implementing these strategies, you can maximize your productivity during your daily big three and make steady progress toward achieving your goals.

Celebrating Your Daily Big Three Accomplishments

Did you know that your brain cannot simultaneously experience gratitude, celebration, and fear? Engaging in gratitude and celebration triggers a neurochemical cocktail that boosts focus, clarity, and energy for the next two hours. This is the power of celebration, and it's a daily call to arms to recognize and celebrate your daily big three accomplishments.

Here are some ideas for celebrating the completion of your daily big three:

- **Gratitude journaling:** Take a few minutes to write down three things you're grateful for related to your accomplishments. Reflecting on your achievements and expressing gratitude can help reinforce positive feelings and motivate you to continue making progress.

- **Treat yourself:** Indulge in a small reward for completing your tasks, such as enjoying a favorite snack, treating yourself to a cup of coffee or tea, or taking a short break to listen to your favorite music or podcast.

- **Physical activity:** Get moving and celebrate with some physical activity. Take a short walk outside, do a quick workout, or stretch to release any tension and boost your energy levels.

- **Share your success:** Celebrate with others by sharing your accomplishments with a friend, family member, or colleague. Celebrating together can increase feelings of connection and support, and receiving positive feedback can reinforce your sense of achievement.

- **Visual reminders:** Create visual reminders of your achievements by writing them on sticky notes and displaying them in a prominent place, or creating a checklist to track your progress over time. Seeing your accomplishments visually can serve as a powerful motivator and reminder of your capabilities.

Take a moment to reflect on your accomplishments and plan for the next day. Celebrate your progress, identify any challenges or lessons learned, and set intentions for the tasks you'll tackle tomorrow. Susan took each task on her post-its and ceremoniously put them in a big jar after she completed them daily. She could literally SEE her dreams come to life, one post-it at a time!

Remember, the key is to choose celebrations that resonate with you and make you feel good. Experiment with different ideas until you find what works best for you, and don't forget to celebrate your daily wins regularly to maintain momentum and motivation on your journey toward achieving your goals.

Don't forget to celebrate your daily wins regularly to maintain momentum and motivation.

What will your celebration look like? It could be a simple act of gratitude, picking some flowers, enjoying a cup of tea, or even doing a little dance. The key is consistency and taking a moment to pause, recognize your accomplishment, and then continue with your day.

This habit of celebrating creates speed in your progress. In your brain, it creates a neurochemical cocktail that allows even more focus and momentum. It's tempting to rush from one task to the next, but by doing so, you're leaving valuable momentum on the table. So choose in advance how you'll celebrate your daily big three, and make it a non-negotiable part of your routine. Now create yours!

Here is my List of Celebrations:

- Write three gratitude points in my journal.
- Enjoy a special cup of tea or coffee.
- Take a short walk outside.
- Share my progress with a friend or family member.
- Create a visual reminder of my achievement.

MOMENTUM TOWARD YOUR DREAMS

You're now in the groove of Brain Priming, using the Mind Matrix, and implementing the 67-Day Year method. As you gain clarity and remove the stories that have been holding you back, you'll start to see real progress.

Momentum begins with consistently completing and celebrating your *daily big three*. But what about the rest of your day? If you have more time, take a few more post-its off the wall and tackle those too. Celebrate each set of three you complete, and you'll find yourself collapsing multiple days' worth of accomplishments into a single day.

By consistently finishing and celebrating your daily big three tasks, you're like a snowball rolling downhill, gaining momentum as you go. This momentum makes it easier to keep going and tackle even bigger tasks. It's like how pushing a heavy object gets easier once it starts moving.

Neuroscience shows that when you achieve small goals and celebrate them, your brain releases chemicals that make you feel good and motivated to keep going. This is similar to how hitting milestones in a video game can make you want to play more. Scripture also talks about the power of momentum, saying, "Let us not become weary in doing good, for at the proper time we will reap a harvest if we do not give up" (Galatians 6:9).

By consistently completing and celebrating your daily big three, you're not only building momentum but also setting yourself up for even greater success in the future. Keep going, and you'll be amazed at how much you can accomplish!

Of course, life happens. There will be days when unexpected events throw you off course. But that's the beauty of the 67-Day Year system: you've already made significant progress with your daily big three, so you can afford to take a step back when needed. On the days when everything goes smoothly, you might complete six, nine, or even more tasks, further accelerating your progress toward your goals.

By focusing on your daily big three, you've already made considerable progress, even if things don't go as planned.

Life is full of surprises, and sometimes unexpected events can throw a wrench into our plans. But here's the great part about the system we're using: by focusing on your *daily big three*, you've already made considerable progress, even if things don't go as planned.

It's crucial to be adaptable and willing to adjust your daily big three as priorities and circumstances change. This flexibility allows you to stay on track even when life gets hectic. On days when everything goes smoothly, you might find yourself completing more than expected, which only accelerates your progress toward your goals. So remember to stay nimble and open to change—it's all part of the journey to success!

This is how you achieve time freedom and create a year's worth of goals in just 67 days. Keep up the momentum, and you'll be amazed at how quickly your dreams become reality.

14

Valuing Time Over All Else

When we think about our dreams and the difference we want to make, it often boils down to three important things: time, energy, and money. Take a moment to reflect on your Brain Prime. Did you notice how money, energy, and the value of time are all connected? For instance, having enough money can give us the freedom to spend time with loved ones, go on vacations, or make a positive impact on others.

Let's break it down further. Imagine you want to start your own business. To do that, you need the time to work on your business idea, the energy to stay focused and motivated, and the finances to invest in your venture. If you're lacking in any of these areas, it can affect your ability to achieve your goal. For example, if you're working a demanding job that drains your energy and leaves you with little free time, it might be challenging to pursue your entrepreneurial dreams. Similarly, if you're struggling financially, it can limit your options and make it harder to dedicate time and energy to your goals.

On the other hand, when these resources are in balance, they can complement each other and propel you forward. For instance, if you have enough money saved up, you might be able to reduce your working hours or even quit your job to focus on your passion project, giving you more time and energy to dedicate to it. Likewise, if you prioritize self-care and manage your energy well, you'll have the stamina to pursue your goals with enthusiasm and resilience, even when faced with obstacles.

If you prioritize self-care and manage your energy well, you'll have the stamina to pursue your goals with enthusiasm and resilience.

Time, energy, and finances are closely intertwined, and finding the right balance among them is key to achieving your aspirations. By understanding how these resources interact and making intentional choices to manage them effectively, you can create the space and opportunity to pursue your dreams and make a meaningful impact in the world.

TIME: THE MOST PRECIOUS RESOURCE

Of all these resources, time is the most precious. Unlike money and energy, which can be replenished, time is finite. We've all wished for more time or the ability to slow it down. As a parent of teenagers, I've realized that time with them is fleeting. They grow up, and their needs and desires evolve.

I remember one particular moment when my son asked me to play catch with him in the backyard. At first, I hesitated, thinking about all the other things I needed to do. But then I realized that these moments wouldn't last forever. So I put aside my to-do list and spent that time with him. It was a simple game of catch, but it meant the world to both of us. That experience taught me to cherish every moment I have with my children, even the seemingly insignificant ones.

As parents, we often get caught up in the busyness of life, juggling work, household chores, and other responsibilities. But it's essential to prioritize quality time with our loved ones. One tip I've found helpful is to schedule regular family activities or outings, whether it's a movie night at home, a hike in the mountains, or a weekend getaway. These moments create lasting memories and strengthen our bonds with each other.

Another idea is to make the most of everyday moments, such as mealtimes or bedtime routines, by turning them into opportunities for connection and conversation. Put away your phones and other distractions and focus on being present with your family. Ask about their day, share stories, and listen attentively to what they have to say. These simple gestures can make a big difference in building strong relationships and creating a sense of belonging.

In the end, it's not about how much time we have but how we choose to spend it. By valuing and prioritizing time with our loved ones, we can create meaningful experiences and cultivate deeper connections that will last a lifetime.

The Value of Meaningful Moments

The moments when we're with the right people, doing what we're meant to do, are when time feels most valuable. It's as if time stands still or flies by because we're fully engaged in life's meaningful experiences.

But in today's fast-paced world, managing time can be tough. Balancing work, family, personal interests, and social life can feel like a juggling act. With technology blurring the lines between work and home, it's hard to switch off and take a break. This can lead to feeling stressed out and strained in our relationships.

Another challenge is making time for ourselves and the things we love. In the midst of our busy lives, we often forget to take care of our own well-being and pursue activities that bring us happiness. Ignoring self-care can leave us feeling drained and overwhelmed.

Plus, there's the pressure to always be achieving something. We might feel guilty when we're not being productive or reaching our goals as quickly as we'd like. This pressure can make us doubt ourselves and feel like we're not good enough.

To find a good balance, we need to set boundaries, prioritize our time, and focus on what's really important to us. By taking care of ourselves, managing our time wisely, and being mindful of our goals, we can handle life's challenges better and make room for the moments that truly count.

To find a good balance, we need to set boundaries, prioritize our time, and focus on what's really important to us.

179

This is why the 67-Day Year method exists. Through the 67-Day Year, Robin learned to identify and replace limiting beliefs that weren't serving her. She noticed shifts like feeling more relaxed, being able to show up to calls focused on serving rather than worrying about the outcome, and taking steps that will eventually bring her boulder goal to fruition, even if more slowly than planned. The process helped Robin gain confidence and make meaningful progress.

The 67-Day Year method is like a roadmap for making the most out of our time.

The 67-Day Year method is like a roadmap for making the most out of our time. It helps us focus on what really matters by breaking down our big goals into smaller steps. By doing just three important tasks each day, we make steady progress toward our goals without feeling overwhelmed.

This method teaches us to organize our tasks based on what's most important for our long-term success. It helps us stay focused on activities that align with our goals, instead of getting distracted by less important things. By sticking to our *daily big three*, we build momentum and get closer to our goals over time.

Using the 67-Day Year method also helps us become more disciplined with our time. By committing to completing just three tasks every day for 67 days, we develop a routine that keeps us on track. This helps us make the most of our time and live a more satisfying life.

Ultimately, the 67-Day Year method shows us how to manage our time wisely, leading to greater success and happiness in the long run. It's not just about making money or generating energy; it's about using our brains to collapse time. It's about stepping into our God-given calling and creating a lasting legacy with our time.

EMBRACING THE ECONOMY OF SPEED

In today's fast-paced world, where artificial intelligence (AI) is transforming the job market, speed is of the essence. I'm using an AI tool to write this book, translating my spoken words into text. This is a testament to the economy of speed we're living in.

Technology plays a vital role in what I call the "economy of speed." With innovations like AI, tasks that used to take hours can now be completed in minutes. This not only changes how we work but also how we perceive time.

AI tools, like being able to speak and have it translated via AI, streamline processes and boost efficiency. They allow us to accomplish tasks faster, freeing up time for other important activities. By leveraging technology, we can maximize productivity and stay ahead in our fast-paced world.

However, it's essential to strike a balance between embracing technology and maintaining human connection. While AI can help us save time, it's crucial not to let it consume us entirely. We must use technology as a tool to enhance our lives, not as a replacement for genuine human interaction.

In essence, technology has reshaped the economy of speed, but it's up to us to harness its power wisely. By embracing technological advancements while prioritizing meaningful connections, we can thrive in our fast-paced world.

Sticking to old ways won't help us achieve our goals. We need to speed things up. That's where the 67-Day Year method and the SINC Neuro Coaching Model come in—they're all about making the most of our time so we can focus on what really matters: spending time with loved ones, helping others, enjoying vacations, and chasing our dreams.

Take a moment to think about your own goals and how you manage your time. Are there ways you could be more efficient? Are you spending enough time on things that make you happy? By asking yourself these questions, you can find ways to improve how you manage your time and make the most of every day.

EMBRACING GOD'S PLAN

In the beginning, God created man and woman and placed them in a perfect environment. Although this book won't delve into what happened afterward, it's clear that God's original plan for us was good. He gave us a powerful brain and a path to follow, with both scripture and science guiding us to make the most of our time.

Now it's your turn to seize control of your time and embrace the principles outlined in the 67-Day Year method. By doing so, you can unlock the full potential that God has bestowed upon you. With determination and faith, you can embark on a journey of transformation, moving ever closer to the life you've always envisioned.

15

Bridging Science and Spirituality

A profound revelation struck me during my Ph.D. studies: the ancient scriptures of the Bible, long a source of spiritual closeness with God for me, began to morph into something even more significant—a guide, a manifesto, a roadmap for navigating life itself.

As I delved deeper into my journey of faith and understanding, I encountered a striking truth that reshaped my worldview. While the Bible had always been a cornerstone for strength, guidance, and a deeper connection with God, it revealed itself anew as a comprehensive guide. This wasn't just spiritual nourishment; it was a manifesto for living, a detailed map through life's complexities.

Albert Einstein once said, "Science without religion is lame, religion without science is blind." This statement resonated

> "Science without religion is lame, religion without science is blind."
>
> —Albert Einstein

deeply, capturing the essence of the revelation that unfolded within me. It highlighted a beautiful, intricate dance between spirituality and science—a synergy that became undeniably clear in my walk with God. Science endeavors to unravel the mysteries of the physical world, while spirituality urges us to look beyond the tangible—to the values and principles that guide our lives and define our eternal journey.

This epiphany was not merely academic; it was a soul-stirring, life-altering realization that bridged what I had previously seen as two distinct realms: the empirical and the spiritual. I came to understand that seeking knowledge, whether through the lens of science or the depth of spirituality, is not an either–or proposition. Both pursuits are quests for truth. Science explains the "how," while spirituality illuminates the "why."

> Science explains the "how," while spirituality illuminates the "why."

Integrating this understanding of the harmony between spirituality and science into my life and ministry has not only broadened my comprehension but also deepened my appreciation for the myriad ways God reveals His truth. This insight—that science and spirituality complement rather than conflict with each other—has become a cornerstone of my teaching. It underscores that our pursuit of knowledge, underpinned by faith, enriches our understanding of God's creation and His intentions for us.

Embracing this blend of spiritual and empirical wisdom encourages us to live fuller, more meaningful lives, grounded in faith yet open to discovery. It serves as a reminder that in our quest for understanding, we are never alone. God guides us through both the seen and the unseen, in our pursuit of knowledge and in our spiritual journey.

The beauty of how Scripture intertwines with the revelations of brain science is particularly striking. Consider this: God created humanity, male and female, and saw that it was good. He charged them to multiply, fill the earth, and govern it. Often, this is interpreted as dominion over the physical world, but through my studies, I saw it as so much more—it's about taking authority over our minds. This interpretation invites us to explore not just the physical dominion but also the mental and spiritual authority that we are endowed with, which can be profoundly empowering.

UNDERSTANDING DIVINE MANDATE: TAKING AUTHORITY OVER OUR MINDS

Taking authority over our minds is a fundamental principle deeply embedded in biblical teachings, which stress the importance of vigilance, discipline, and positivity in our thought processes. Scriptures such as Romans 12:2 ("Do not conform to the pattern of this world, but be transformed by the renewing of your mind.") and Philippians 4:8 ("Finally, brothers and sisters, whatever is true, whatever is noble, whatever is right, whatever is pure, whatever is lovely, whatever is admirable—if anything is excellent or praiseworthy—think about such things.") clearly articulate the significance of aligning our thoughts with godly values and principles.

This biblical perspective dovetails remarkably with scientific understandings of the brain, particularly through concepts like neuroplasticity and cognitive behavioral therapy (CBT). Neuroplasticity, which is the brain's capacity to form new neural connections throughout life, supports the notion that our mental practices—such as maintaining focus on positive, noble, and pure thoughts—can physically reshape our brain's structure and function. This scientific principle bolsters the biblical injunction to renew our minds, demonstrating that engaging in positive, scripture-aligned thought patterns can effect lasting changes in our brain architecture, enhancing our capacity for positivity, resilience, and godly discernment.

CBT, a well-established psychological treatment, complements these teachings by illustrating how our thoughts directly influence our emotions and behaviors. CBT's methodology involves identifying and challenging negative and unhelpful thought patterns to transform our emotional responses and behaviors. This process mirrors the biblical exhortation to focus on what is true, noble, right, and pure. The scientific validation of CBT underscores the biblical view that controlling our thoughts is pivotal to our emotional well-being and spiritual health.

Moreover, studies in the field of positive psychology reinforce these connections, showing that gratitude, optimism, and forgiveness—themes prevalent in biblical teachings—profoundly impact our psychological well-being, social relationships, and even physical health. These findings lend scientific support to the biblical assertion that cultivating a positive, God-centered mindset is not only spiritually enriching but also beneficial to overall health.

The biblical mandate to take authority over our minds is robustly supported by scientific research into brain function and psychology. Both the spiritual discipline of renewing our minds according to God's word and scientific practices aimed at reshaping our thought patterns demonstrate the profound impact of mind control in achieving a balanced, healthy, and fulfilling life. This convergence of biblical wisdom and scientific understanding highlights the holistic nature of human well-being, encompassing both our spiritual and mental health.

God, our Creator, designed us to be creators ourselves. His declaration that His creation was "good" was an affirmation of our inherent capability and calling. We are meant to fill the earth and exercise authority, not just over the physical elements but, crucially, over our thoughts. This insight has transformed my understanding of the Bible from merely a spiritual text to a powerful blueprint for harnessing our minds' potential.

The ancient scriptures of the Bible serve as a fundamental blueprint for mastering control over one's mind.

The ancient scriptures of the Bible, filled with wisdom and guidance, serve as a fundamental blueprint for mastering control over one's mind. The teachings on thought life, emotional regulation, and personal discipline within these texts have profound parallels with modern psychological principles. By integrating specific biblical examples with contemporary scientific findings, we gain a deeper appreciation of the timeless relevance of these ancient scriptures in promoting mental and emotional well-being.

The Power of Positive Thinking

Philippians 4:8 encourages us to focus our thoughts on things that are true, noble, right, pure, lovely, and admirable—anything excellent or praiseworthy. This scripture isn't just a call to positivity but a strategic guide for mental conditioning.

This directive aligns seamlessly with the concept of cognitive restructuring in CBT, where the focus is on identifying and transforming negative thought patterns into positive ones. Positive psychology also supports this, highlighting the significant impact of positive thinking on mental health, resilience, and overall wellbeing.

Renewing the Mind

Romans 12:2 challenges us not to conform to the world's pattern but to be transformed by renewing our minds. This process of renewal is essential for spiritual and psychological growth.

This principle mirrors the concept of neuroplasticity—the brain's capability to reorganize itself by forming new neural connections throughout life. Engaging in practices like mindfulness and cognitive-behavioral therapy can catalyze this transformation, altering our thought patterns, emotional responses, and behaviors in profound ways.

Managing Anxiety through Mindfulness and Prayer

Philippians 4:6–7 teaches us not to be anxious but to present our requests to God with thanksgiving, assuring that the peace of God will guard our hearts and minds.

This scripture parallels mindfulness and stress reduction techniques commonly used in psychology to manage anxiety. The practice of prayer and presenting concerns with gratitude can be likened to mindfulness meditation, which fosters present-moment awareness and a nonjudgmental acceptance of thoughts and feelings, leading to decreased stress and a greater sense of peace.

Self-Control and Discipline

2 Timothy 1:7 states that God has given us a spirit not of fear but of power, love, and a sound mind—a directive that emphasizes the virtues of self-control and mental discipline.

The notion of a "sound mind" reflects the psychological understanding of executive functions, which include working memory, flexible thinking, and self-control. Studies in psychology have shown that enhancing these executive functions can significantly improve decision-making, problem-solving, and emotional regulation capabilities.

These biblical teachings, viewed through the lens of modern psychology, reveal how ancient wisdom can guide contemporary practices in mental health and personal growth. The alignment between these teachings and scientific understanding highlights the holistic nature of human well-being, integrating spiritual, emotional, and psychological dimensions.

When God commands us to multiply and take dominion, it is not only a directive to influence the physical world but also a call to master our thoughts and thereby shape our reality. This understanding underscores our role as creators—mirroring our Creator—in both mental and spiritual capacities. Recognizing that our thoughts have the power to shape our world, experiences, and future is not only empowering but transformative.

The Path of Illumination

The Bible serves not just as a spiritual guide but as a blueprint for mastering our minds and becoming creators in our own right. Psalm 119:105 ("Your word is a lamp for my feet, a light on my path") illustrates beautifully how divine guidance is meant to illuminate our journey, both immediately and in the broader scope of our lives. Understanding these scriptures as directives for mental and spiritual authority breathes new life into their meanings, showing us the path to a balanced, fulfilling life.

The Power of Belief: Scriptural Insights into Thought Patterns

The teachings of Scripture provide profound insights into the nature of belief and thought patterns that align remarkably well with contemporary brain science, particularly concepts such as Brain Priming in the SINC Neuro Coach model. These practices highlight the transformative power of aligning one's thoughts with God's truths and the principles of positive psychology and neuroplasticity.

Brain Priming is a technique that involves vividly defining and consistently visualizing the achievement of a goal or the embodiment of a certain trait. In a biblical context, Hebrews 11:1 defines faith as "the assurance of things hoped for, the conviction of things not seen." This perfectly encapsulates the essence of Brain Priming—maintaining a firm belief in God's promises and provisions, even when they are not yet visible in the physical realm. By repeatedly affirming and living out the truths and promises found in Scripture, we engage our minds in a manner that harmonizes with our faith and beliefs.

Additionally, Brain Prime often involves positive, truth-based statements that are spoken or meditated upon. Philippians 4:8 urges believers to focus their thoughts on whatever is true, noble, right, pure, lovely, and admirable. Regularly affirming these truths can significantly reshape our thought patterns, aligning them more closely with God's perspective and promises.

INTEGRATING SCRIPTURAL TEACHINGS WITH CONTEMPORARY BRAIN SCIENCE

Neuroplasticity, the brain's ability to form and reorganize synaptic connections, especially in response to learning or experience, is crucial to understanding how we can leverage scriptural truths. When we engage in visualization and affirmations based on scriptural truths, we are essentially using neuroplasticity to "rewire" our brains. This process can strengthen neural pathways associated with positive thinking, faith, and resilience.

For example, visualizing oneself as healed, prosperous, or at peace, in alignment with biblical promises, can create neural pathways that enhance feelings of hope and expectancy. Regularly affirming scriptural truths about one's identity in Christ (e.g., loved, chosen, redeemed) helps counteract negative thought patterns and builds a more positive self-concept.

Scriptural References and
Contemporary Brain Science

Joshua 1:8 emphasizes the importance of meditation on God's Word: "Keep this Book of the Law always on your lips; meditate on it day and night, so that you may be careful to do everything written in it. Then you will be prosperous and successful." This verse highlights the psychological benefits of repetitive positive thinking and its impact on behavior and success.

Proverbs 23:7, "For as he thinks in his heart, so is he," underlines the profound truth that our thoughts shape our reality, mirroring the psychological concept of the self-fulfilling prophecy. Believing positive, God-aligned truths about ourselves can lead to behaviors and outcomes that reflect those beliefs.

HARNESSING DIVINE INSTRUCTION
FOR MENTAL MASTERY

This exploration of scriptural wisdom and brain science is not just about understanding our mental capabilities; it's about recognizing the divine guidance embedded within the scriptures. These ancient texts serve not only as sources for spiritual communion but also as instructions on how to harness the power God has given us over our minds. They teach us how to be creators, to take authority over our cognitive processes, and to shape our lives in the image of our divine potential.

CONQUERING FEAR: BIBLICAL AND NEUROSCIENTIFIC PERSPECTIVES

One of the most emphasized commands in the Bible, mentioned an astounding 360 times, is to fear not. This directive transcends a comforting suggestion; it is a critical instruction that reveals a profound truth about the power of our thoughts. Fear is not just an emotion but a mental pathway that can dominate our brains, obstructing our ability to hold onto faith. When God instructs us not to fear, He is essentially advising us to choose our thoughts wisely, for they have the power to shape our reality.

Fear is not just an emotion but a mental pathway that can dominate our brains.

Scriptures such as Isaiah 41:10 ("So do not fear, for I am with you; do not be dismayed, for I am your God.") and Joshua 1:9 ("Have I not commanded you? Be strong and courageous. Do not be afraid; do not be discouraged, for the Lord your God will be with you wherever you go.") provide potent reminders of the spiritual resources available to believers facing fear. The biblical narrative encourages turning to faith and divine assurance as mechanisms to manage and redirect fear, suggesting a deep understanding of fear as a controllable thought pattern.

From a neuroscientific view, fear originates in the amygdala, a part of the brain responsible for emotional processing. When faced with a perceived threat, the amygdala triggers a fight-or-flight response that, while essential for survival, can become maladaptive in situations of chronic fear or perceived threats. This often leads to anxiety, stress, and impaired decision-making.

Over time, chronic fear can even rewire the brain, strengthening neural pathways associated with fear and making one more susceptible to anxiety and fear-based responses in the future.

The biblical command not to fear aligns with cognitive restructuring, a key component of cognitive-behavioral therapy, which involves identifying, challenging, and replacing fear-based thoughts with more rational and balanced ones. This parallels the scriptural encouragement to replace fear with faith, trust, and reliance on God's presence and promises. Moreover, modern research into neuroplasticity—the brain's ability to form new neural connections—supports the idea that focusing consistently on faith over fear can literally change the brain's structure and function. This scientific insight provides a biological basis for the scriptural practice of meditating on God's word and promises as a strategy for overcoming fear.

Thus, each day we are presented with a choice: will it be faith or fear? Both are forms of belief, and within the context of the STEBDAR model, they represent the B—the belief that we automate. Scriptures are not merely words for spiritual communion; they are a manifesto for life, guiding us to take every thought captive, renew our minds, and align our thinking with faith over fear. The Bible tells us to focus on what is good, true, pure, and praiseworthy—there's no room for shadows or fear in this mindset.

By intentionally shifting our focus from fear to faith, we engage in a process of rewiring our brains, aligning our thoughts with the positive, the possible, and the God-ordained. This isn't just spiritual; it's neuroscientific, demonstrating that these teachings are practical instructions for mental mastery. As creators, God has given us the authority and the tools to shape our thoughts and, consequently, our lives. He reveals that the key to fulfilling our calling and living a heaven-on-earth existence lies within the power of our minds. This is the essence of taking dominion—not just over the physical world but over our internal landscapes, making "renewing our minds" a neurological as well as a spiritual exercise.

RENEWING THE MIND: A SPIRITUAL AND NEUROLOGICAL PROCESS

We have the power to reshape our thought patterns, to automate positivity and faith in our subconscious. This is where our creative power is ignited—we have the authority to choose which thoughts enter our subconscious and which ones are discarded. This process of mental renewal aligns our thoughts with those of Christ. He doesn't entertain fear. He believes without needing to see. This is the mindset we're called to embrace.

The process of mind renewal is a transformative journey that encompasses both spiritual and neurological dimensions. From a spiritual (biblical) perspective, mind renewal is about aligning one's thoughts and attitudes with God's will, as articulated in Romans 12:2, which urges believers not to conform to the patterns of this world but to be transformed by the renewing of their minds. This transformation allows individuals to discern and embrace what is good, pleasing, and perfect in the eyes of God. Spiritually, this process involves engaging with Scripture, prayer, meditation, and other practices that focus the mind on divine truths and principles.

Neurologically, the concept of mind renewal finds a parallel in the principle of neuroplasticity, which refers to the brain's remarkable ability to reorganize itself by forming new neural connections throughout life. This ability underlines the brain's capacity to adapt and change in response to new experiences, thoughts, and environments. Neuroplasticity shows us that habitual patterns of thought and behavior can indeed be altered, which means that with intentional practice, individuals can cultivate new, more positive ways of thinking and responding to the world around them.

Neuroplasticity illustrates how repeated mental activities, such as focused thought, prayer, or meditation, can physically change the structure of the brain. For example, engaging in regular meditation has been shown to increase the thickness of the prefrontal cortex, an area associated with attention, decision-making, and self-regulation. Similarly, prayer and meditation can enhance connectivity in the brain regions involved in self-awareness, compassion, and introspective thinking.

Prayer and meditation can enhance connectivity in the brain regions involved in self-awareness, compassion, and introspective thinking.

These neurological changes reflect the spiritual process of mind renewal by demonstrating how consistent engagement with spiritual practices can lead to substantive, measurable changes in the brain. These changes, in turn, can influence an individual's thought patterns, emotional responses, and behaviors, aligning them more closely with spiritual virtues and values.

HOW SPIRITUAL PRACTICES
FACILITATE MIND RENEWAL

Spiritual practices such as prayer and meditation are pivotal in facilitating the renewal of the mind. Prayer allows individuals to communicate with God, express their desires for transformation, and receive divine guidance. It centers the mind on God's promises and faithfulness, reinforcing a deep-seated trust and reliance on Him. Similarly, meditation, particularly on Scripture, aids in internalizing God's Word, embedding its truths deeply within one's consciousness.

These practices are not only spiritual but have tangible neurological benefits. They contribute to the rewiring of the brain by reinforcing neural pathways associated with positive emotions, compassion, and spiritual connectedness. As these pathways are strengthened, individuals are more likely to exhibit attitudes and behaviors that reflect their spiritual values. This demonstrates the tangible impact of mind renewal on daily life and underscores the powerful interplay between faith and science. It reveals how spiritual practices endorsed by Scripture can lead to significant neurological changes, facilitating a transformative process that aligns individuals more closely with divine principles and values. This harmonious relationship between the spiritual and the scientific provides a comprehensive approach to personal growth and spiritual development, emphasizing the holistic nature of human transformation.

Proverbs offers a powerful insight: "As a man or woman thinks, so he or she will become." This statement is not merely poetic; it's a neurological truth. Our thoughts are the architects of our reality. Each thought we entertain lays a brick in the construction of our future. There is no neutral ground; we are either building a future based on the repetition of our past experiences or creating a new path forward. If we dwell on fear, doubt, and negativity, that becomes the reality we manifest. Conversely, when we focus on faith, positivity, and God's promises, we create a life that reflects those beliefs.

The directive to "think on what is good, true, pure, praise-worthy" is not just an encouragement toward positivity—it's a command to focus our minds on constructive, faith-filled thoughts, actively dispelling the shadows of fear. This is the essence of taking dominion over our thoughts, of being creators in the truest sense. We are called to align our thoughts with our divine purpose, renewing our minds to manifest the life God intends for us—a life marked by abundance, creativity, and ful-fillment. By focusing our thoughts on these positive aspects, we train our brains to look for the good, to anticipate success, and to synchronize with God's promises.

And here's where it becomes truly magnificent. In these practices, there is no shadow, no trace of fear. This is God's way of empowering us, affirming that we are creators at our core. He commands us not merely to suggest but to take domin-ion over our minds, to renew our thinking daily, and to align our thoughts with His. We are to submit every thought to the authority of Christ, aligning with our calling, our gifts, and the purpose of our lives. When we focus on what is true, pure, and praiseworthy, we step out of the shadows of fear and into the light of faith.

I bring this to you with a sense of urgency and excitement. It's time to grasp the depth of God's love, His passion, and His desire for us to succeed, to be the best versions of ourselves, and to step fully into our calling. This is about more than just personal achievement; it's about manifesting heaven on earth, about living in a way that honors the Creator. We are here to reflect God's ways on earth, to be active creators in His image. Remember, when God looked at His creation, He declared it is "good."

EMBRACING OUR ROLE
AS CREATORS

Embrace this truth with all your heart: think on things that are good, true, pure, and praiseworthy. Let these become the pillars of your thoughts and watch as your life transforms, aligning with the heavenly blueprint designed for you. This is not just an encouragement; it is your divine mandate, your call to bring the kingdom of heaven to the here and now.

As we conclude this exploration of the profound connections between spirituality, neuroscience, and the transformative power of mind renewal, we return to a foundational truth: we are creators, made in the image of the Creator. This identity is not merely symbolic; it is a call to action, an invitation to embrace our inherent ability to shape our realities, influence our thoughts and behaviors, and ultimately align our lives with our divine purpose.

> *We are creators, made in the image of the Creator.*

The insights and tools discussed in this chapter—from the biblical principles of mind renewal to the scientific revelations about neuroplasticity—equip us with a deeper understanding of how we can actively participate in the transformation of our own lives. They remind us that we are not passive observers in our journey but active participants, empowered by our Creator to make choices that foster growth, healing, and alignment with our highest selves.

Embracing our role as creators means recognizing the power of our thoughts, the impact of our beliefs, and the significance of our actions. It involves a deliberate effort to renew our minds, to replace fear with faith, and to cultivate thoughts and habits that reflect the love, wisdom, and creativity of the God in whose image we are made. This process of renewal is not a one-time event but a lifelong journey, one that requires persistence, patience, and, above all, faith in the transformative power of God's presence in our lives.

As you move forward, use the tools and insights provided in this chapter as a compass. Let them guide you in your quest for personal transformation and spiritual alignment. Engage in practices that nurture your mind, body, and spirit. Spend time in prayer and meditation, reflecting on God's Word and its relevance to your life. Seek to understand the neurological underpinnings of your thought patterns and behaviors; embrace the practices that promote positive change.

Remember, you are a creator, endowed with the capacity to bring forth life, beauty, and goodness in a world that yearns for the touch of the divine. By aligning your life with your divine purpose, you not only transform yourself but also contribute to the transformation of the world around you. Let this knowledge inspire you to take bold steps toward renewal and to live each day as a testament to the creative power that resides within you.

And now, we arrive at the pièce de résistance: God's promise that He will give us more than we can ever ask or imagine! This promise is not just a comforting thought; it's a fundamental principle that intersects with the science we've explored. It's a divine assertion that our potential is boundless when aligned with His will. This profound truth was hidden in ancient texts, waiting for us to uncover and fully understand its implications. It's God's way of saying that when we align our thoughts and actions with His divine order, He unlocks possibilities beyond our wildest dreams.

As I wrap up this section, my heart is full because I'm not just sharing brain science and success strategies; I'm sharing a divine mystery. In the coming chapters, we'll delve into practical tools for success, but for now, I want you to bask in the awe and wonder of being a creator, made in the image of the ultimate Creator. Embrace the power to take authority over your mind, to cast out fear, to meditate on what is good, true, pure, and lovely. This isn't just about achieving goals; it's about submitting your daily thoughts to the higher purpose God has for you, bringing a slice of heaven to earth.

So, as we move forward, let your heart swell with excitement. Realize that Scripture has always been the roadmap, showing us "the way to walk in it." We're not just reading metaphorical wisdom; we're discovering a manifesto for living a heavenly life on earth. By embracing this divine blueprint, we honor our Creator and utilize the gifts, talents, and skills He's entrusted to us, making a real impact on the world.

> Scripture has always been the roadmap, showing us "the way to walk in it."

Conclusion

A Life by Design

God didn't create you by default; He created you with intention. He equipped you with a brain and provided the blueprint through scriptures and scientific principles, not just to react to the world but to be a creator, like Him. In the scriptures, it says God made humanity in His image, as creators. He's instilled in you the desires of your heart and given you the tools to bring them to life. Your thoughts, shaped by this divine influence, have the power to create your reality.

According to the teachings found in scriptures, when God made humanity, He gave us special abilities that reflect His own. It's like He made us to be mini-creators, capable of shaping our lives and the world around us. This means we're not just passive beings; we have the power to make things happen. The desires we feel deep in our hearts aren't random—they're there for a reason. It's like God planted them inside us to guide us toward our purpose in life. And when we focus on these desires and believe in them, it's like we're tapping into a special energy that helps us turn our dreams into reality. Scriptures also tell us that our thoughts are super important. They have the power to shape our lives. So, when we fill our minds with positive thoughts and trust in God's plan, it's like we're creating a path for good things to happen in our lives.

In simple terms, the teachings in scriptures tell us that we have the power to create the life we want by focusing on our dreams, trusting in God, and keeping our thoughts positive.

THE 1 PERCENT DIFFERENCE

Recent research in DNA sequencing has revealed that we are all 99 percent identical in our genetic makeup. It's the 1 percent that makes each of us unique. This 1 percent is your unique contribution to the world, your individuality ordained by God. If we don't express this 1 percent, it dies with us, making the graveyard the richest place on Earth with unfulfilled potential.

Scientific studies have delved into the significance of this 1 percent difference, revealing how variations in genetic code can influence everything from physical characteristics to cognitive abilities. This small percentage plays a pivotal role in shaping our talents, skills, and unique contributions to the world. Embracing and celebrating this diversity enriches our collective experience and fosters a deeper understanding of what it means to be human.

Embracing and celebrating this diversity enriches our collective experience and fosters a deeper understanding of what it means to be human.

Your 1 percent is crucial. Your dreams, your vision, your calling—they all matter. My hope is that this book serves not just as a source of information, but as a life manifesto.

A manifesto is like a personal declaration of beliefs, values, and intentions. It's a document that reflects who you are and what you stand for, guiding your actions and decisions in life. In the context of this book, it's about defining your purpose, clarifying your goals, and committing to living according to your highest ideals.

This book serves as a manifesto by offering readers a framework and tools to uncover their deepest desires, set meaningful goals, and take deliberate steps toward realizing their dreams. Through various exercises, insights, and practical advice, you are encouraged to explore your values, identify your passions, and align your actions with your aspirations.

By doing so, you'll get clearer on what you want out of life, create a plan for getting there, and build habits that help you reach your goals. It's all about living your life on purpose and making your dreams come true, based on what matters most to you.

COLLAPSING TIME AND CREATING A LEGACY

Consider your life as it is now and imagine it transformed into something even greater. What if you could collapse time, achieving more in a year than you ever thought possible? This book is your guide to doing just that, to creating a 67-Day Year where each day is filled with purpose, progress, and fulfillment.

As you read through the pages and engage with the exercises, take time to reflect on your own life. What legacy do you want to leave behind? How do you want to impact future generations? Think about your deepest desires and aspirations. Then, consider how the principles outlined in this book can help you design a life that aligns with your unique purpose.

By applying the strategies and techniques shared here, you can begin to reshape your reality, moving closer to the life you envision for yourself and those you care about. It's about taking intentional steps each day to build a legacy that will endure long after you're gone. So, are you ready to start living a life that leaves a lasting impact?

Are you ready to start living a life that leaves a lasting impact?

EMBRACING YOUR UNIQUE POTENTIAL

Now it's your turn. Unleash your 1 percent to the world, create a legacy that endures through time. You are the creator of your thoughts, and your thoughts have the power to shape your future.

Now is the moment to tap into the unparalleled power that resides within you and unleash it upon the world. You possess a unique gift, your 1 percent, waiting to ignite a legacy that transcends time itself. Your thoughts, dreams, and actions possess the potential to sculpt a future of boundless possibility and enduring impact.

I implore you to heed the call today. Utilize the tools and wisdom bestowed upon you in these pages to craft a life that mirrors your deepest passions and loftiest aspirations. Embrace your role as the architect of your destiny and let the brilliance of your 1 percent illuminate the world.

Believe, with unwavering conviction, in your capacity for greatness beyond measure. Take bold and decisive action, and witness as your legacy unfurls in magnificent splendor. The world eagerly awaits the unparalleled gifts and contributions that only you can offer. Now is the time to step into your divine destiny and forge a life of unparalleled significance. Are you prepared to answer the call and embark on this extraordinary life? Creating your LIFE by DESIGN!

Go ahead, flip your brain's success switch on, and change the world!

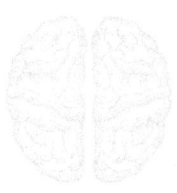

Acknowledgments

To my children, Max and Jordan—you inspire me every single day of my life to be better than the day before. You gave me the fuel to dream—not for me, but for you to see anything was possible.

To my husband, Micah, my rock and my true love—you've always believed in me!

Thank You JESUS for saving me and giving me this calling that helps people break chains and get the greatness you planted inside of them out to the world!

To my mentors—you helped me to see what was possible before I saw it happen.

To Pat Flynn, thank you for always helping me to see what I couldn't so that I could create what I have.

To Russell Brunson, for always mapping out the steps and the mindset to serve at the deepest level!

To Brooke Thomas, for always being the example of how to honor God with your business and life!

To Shanda Sumpter, for always pushing me to the next version of me!

To James Wedmore, for always being an example of deep and authentic coaching and overdelivering!

To Jasmine Star, for helping me see the unique sauce I bring to the world and helping me get it out in a powerful way!

To Amy Porterfield, for always believing that what I created had to get in front of people and showing me the steps to do it!

To the most amazing friends—Christina Jandali, Jennifer Allwood, and Dana Malstaff—who have been with me beside me and encouraging me every step of the way!

Thank you for always reminding me to do the work and change the world!

About the Author

D r. Shannon Irvine is a neuropsychologist, entrepreneur, and kingdom-minded CEO who believes success is inevitable when you align your brain, your faith, and your calling.

After years of hustling, burning out, and watching her business plateau despite all the strategy in the world, she discovered the real key to success: rewiring the subconscious patterns that quietly sabotage your growth.

Today, she's the founder of the **67 Day Year™ methods**, the **SINC NeuroCoach™ Certification**, and the creator of several trademarked neuroscience models including the **Mind Matrix™**, **Brain Prime™**, and the proven **SINC NeuroCoach™ Model for**

Transformation. Through these systems, she's helped thousands of entrepreneurs, coaches, and leaders rewire their minds, automate success, and unlock results they once thought impossible.

As a sought-after speaker and high-level coach, Shannon mentors 6- to 8-figure entrepreneurs, CEOs, and industry leaders—helping them break free from hidden limits, reclaim their time, and multiply their impact without sacrificing what matters most.

Her greatest joy comes from watching lives transform—from the CEO who finally scales with ease, to the entrepreneur who unlocks their next million, to the orphaned child in Uganda who finds family again through her nonprofit, **Mosaic Vision.**

Whether on stage, behind a microphone, or guiding world-changers into their next breakthrough, Shannon lives by one truth: **you were made for more—and when your brain is aligned with God's design, success becomes inevitable.**

For more book resources, free extras,
and access to the audio book, scan here:

Or go to

WWW.67DAYYEARBOOK.COM

I would appreciate your feedback on what
chapters helped you most and what you
would like to see in future books.

If you enjoyed this book and found it helpful,
please leave a review on Amazon.

Visit me at

WWW.67DAYYEARBOOK.COM

where you can find additional resources and
videos to walk you through the process.

THANK YOU!

www.ingramcontent.com/pod-product-compliance
Lightning Source LLC
Chambersburg PA
CBHW070815120626
46556CB00002B/506